A REFLECTION OF MY FATHER

ACCEPTING THE PAST, EMBRACING ME & GROWING

A REFLECTION OF MY FATHER

*ACCEPTING THE PAST,
EMBRACING ME & GROWING*

SHAIA L. BERNARD

XULON PRESS

Xulon Press
2301 Lucien Way #415
Maitland, FL 32751
407.339.4217
www.xulonpress.com

© 2019 by Shaia L. Bernard

All rights reserved solely by the author. The author guarantees all contents are original and do not infringe upon the legal rights of any other person or work. No part of this book may be reproduced in any form without the permission of the author. The views expressed in this book are not necessarily those of the publisher.

Unless otherwise indicated, Scripture quotations are taken from the King James Version of the Bible. Public domain.

Printed in the United States of America.

ISBN-13: 978-1-54567-446-8

Dedication

To my
Heavenly and earthly Daddy
For guidance and the will to do
Who unconditionally loved me before I was born
Who protected me, encouraged me, chastised me,
taught me value and worth, and validated me.
Where one cease in physical presence (for our time
runs short) the other continues, greater and eternally.

Thank you for the words you've whispered and the
assurance that I can do anything I aspire. It is because
of you I will do all that I am destined.
I dedicate this to you for loving me.

Table of Contents

Dedication		v
Acknowledgements		ix
Introduction	Why I wrote this	 xi
	For Who Did I Write This?	xiv
Chapter 1	Reflection	1
	The Mirror	4
	Reflections of Reflection	 8
Chapter 2	My Life, My Story	11
	The Outlook	 18
	Reflections of My Life, Your Story	25
Chapter 3	Identity	 29
	What's in a Name	 29
	Shaping My Existence	33
	Face to Face	37
	Okay Being Me	44
	Reflections of Your Identity	46
Chapter 4	Destined a Daughter	51
	I am because I was meant to be	 52

	She Needs Him, He Needs Her 55
	Shaped for Performance 58
	To Become Woman 63
	A Daughter After His Heart 67
	Reflections on Destined a Daughter 71
Chapter 5	A Reflection of His Presence 77
	You were there, and you are still 78
	Reflections of His Presence 83
Chapter 6	A Reflection of His Love 87
	And the Greatest of These 90
	Still looking for His Heart 96
	Reflection on Reflections of His Love 101
Chapter 7	A Reflection from His Validation 105
	Approved for this world 106
	Rejecting Rejection 114
	Reflections from His Validation 119
Epilogue 127
References 135

Acknowledgements

To my husband for his love, patience,
encouragement and annoying persistence
that helped push me to the finish.

To my mother for allowing my father to be
all that he was to us. Only a Woman could allow a
daddy to be present, to love, and validate
his daughter to Womanhood. You are ***Mother***...

To my son for giving me a reason...
To all that contributed to this project in any way,
you know who you are.
From my heart to yours, thank you.

Introduction

Why I wrote this

When I decided to write a book I was at a loss for content. While there is much to be said, I wanted the words stamped across these pages to imbue a spirit of redefining, reflection, restoration and renewal.

Being pressed to write, I gravitated to a topic that's close to my heart, the value of woman. But telling my sisters they are valuable, have purpose, and are loved isn't enough. This adage has tolled in our hearing for decades, as our hearts still struggle to believe that we are enough.

Putting pen to paper, passionate expressions began to well up as I contemplated how to encourage and inspire women to keep pushing, to keep bringing change, to keep moving to destiny. The more I pondered and wrote, the more I was inundated with thoughts of my fathers' impact, and confirmations of this books purpose became finite.

A Reflection of My Father

The timing of this endeavor, and its release, will prove crucial to the current state of female exposition. We are in a state of emergency. Yes, emergency. Across the planes there is an urgent cry that innuendos relief from demanding stresses and unrealistic and unfair expectations of society. In efforts to meet them, we can stifle greater potentiality or lose ourselves in its' acceptance.

My reality is that I am a daughter, and I understand that a daughter's relationship experience with her father impacts how she interprets relationships with her mate, family, friends, co-workers and even how she sees strangers. If he is present, there are opportunities to shape her understanding and thoughts of self and love, through the giving of love and validation. In extended absences she is forced to navigate without his instruction. This issue has proven to be formidable, but one is still able to prevail.

Observance over the years have helped me to realize that there are too many of us hurting, holding on to too much pain, and hiding behind counterfeit smiles, attitudes and isolation. But the eyes speak truths to anyone who is willing to see.

There are many *successful* women who manage family, personal lives, and those who scale the career ladder, and are without financial concerns. But some of these same women struggle with self-esteem and fail to maintain healthy relationships.

Introduction

Too many times I've witnessed us trading our own happiness, worth and precious temples for the pleasure of others. Women are strong, dedicated and fearless. Even when we're frightened, we move with grace through our own hurts and sorrows as we try to heal others.

We carry other people's burdens while masking our own disappointments, but still walk with our shoulders back and heads held high. We love to the end of ourselves, and when it seems we can't do it any longer, we love more.

Without question, we play the most critical part to reaching our fullest potential in love, relationship, vocationally, socially and in life in general.

We seek happiness, need security, even when it's hard to admit, and desire the strength of man that will embrace the gentleness of our womanhood. We want to be loved and live Be**you**tiful lives.

Much of what we experience as women, both positive and negative, are results of decisions we make, regardless of the reasons we blame those decisions on. Those decisions direct us toward our best or not so best lives. It is enlightening when we become aware that many of those decisions were filtered through the smoky lens of a little girl with innocent expectations, believing her daddy was everything, or at least wanting him to be.

In my own life, this ring truer than I can explain. I was a little girl who loved her daddy and knew he would always be there; a young lady, strong and independent, who continued to search for truth, genuineness and for her real place in the world; and a young woman who didn't know how much she needed to experience her father's love, protection, validation and his presence, close-up.

I wasn't aware that I needed to take in all that he was willing to pour into me. And while it is amongst the season clichés, there is a newfound and refreshing outlook when you realize that *you **are** valuable, your body **is** a temple, and you **are** priceless.*

To repeat this profusely is worth its reward, *you **are** valuable, your body **is** a temple, and you **are** priceless.* But it must go beyond reiterating adages and beliefs that vacation on the brains island. It must break through cracks, seep through crevices, and divide to the bones and sinew, to adjoin itself to the fibers of your being.

In other words, it has to be what you know, believe and live.

For Who Did I Write This?

I wrote this book to help us; daughters, mothers, sisters, friends, to understand that in spite of others, we are made for greatness.

This book is written for the ***daughter*** who wants to understand the honor in daughterhood, and how a father reflects her own honor. Daughter, this *is* you.

Introduction

The ***Father***, who need to recognize his impact on his daughter's life, and what she needs from him to shape her future self. Father, this is you. Daughter, this is *for* you.

The ***mother*** who wants her daughter to live her best life, to have a healthy relationship with her father, to teach her to embrace his leading and be the best woman she can be. Mother, this is you. Daughter, this is ***because*** of you.

For ***daughters*** who desire to carefully examine the why of your relationships. A Reflection of My Father helps you to take a closer look and be honest about–you.

It is for ***fathers*** who want to be counted worthy of imparting blessings of identity into the precious jewel they co-created. And, those who want to better understand what their daughters need to thrive in life and in relationship, and to walk with confidence.

It is for ***mothers*** to help you understand what a father daughter relationship should look like. To help us see what we may have missed and to help us, help them be strong, confident women and to nourish their relationship with wisdom and love.

In the pages below, I share memories of my childhood and explain my perspective of them. You'll see how I carried with me certain beliefs and perspectives on life, love and relationships, and what has shaped me to be the beautiful, confident and fulfilled woman I am today and also the one that still has to be intentional about reshaping her life by what she believes to be true along her journey.

I've gathered information and have inquired of multiple women just like us. I've spoken with them on personal levels, through counseling sessions and healing groups, and through personal observation. Summaries of some of these results are threaded through these pages.

These women, including myself, share beliefs, views, and upbringing. We are from various backgrounds, diverse living dynamics, two-parent and single parent homes, children of adoption and those raised in the foster system.

I've heard untold accounts of not being able to let go, of pouring out their hearts to those undeserving, and them wearing masks of shame that shouldn't be theirs.

Their rough exterior seemed impenetrable; their hearts unbreakable. But their reality was that at any moment they *could* break. After so much bending, pulling and stretching, not just their hearts, but they themselves, *could* break.

I wish to take you beyond the presumed fairytales and bring you into today's reality, of young fragile girls living in grown women's bodies, having grown women experiences, and live adult women lives.

This is for you. And for me.

And your sister, mother, friend, and the stranger that sits next to you each day. The one you pass on the street. The one you see at the grocery store. The one at the bank. And every girl and woman you meet anywhere, anytime, anyplace.

I want to encourage you to accept you, your flaws, quirkiness and all you are, so you will live your life, unrestricted.

We go on with our lives doing what we must, but we tend to experience the same mishaps because we haven't received revelation and understanding on the trigger points (the emotional or psychological sources that keeps us bound to a cycle).

When we start recognizing what those trigger points are, we can do something about them. The questions we often ask ourselves, why does this bother me so much? Why do I have an issue with this or them? Why do I keep doing the same thing over and over? Why haven't I moved past this? Why do I keep attracting the same type of people? or any similar questions all can be answered.

I ask that as you read, remain open to what you begin to feel.

At times you may be tempted to immediately deny what's being said. You may not agree with it, or pass it off as someone else's issue, but be open to honest self-examination. But with that, also be cautious of self-criticism, or only identifying with the mistakes of the past. The goal is not to spotlight our faults for condemnation. The aim is to help identify triggers and areas of struggle for healing and growth.

My goal is to help you reflect on your life in a different way. A way that elicits feelings you've ignored and occurrences that have stunted you in areas.

Trigger points can happen as a result of relational absences, abuses and societal mishaps among other things. Once we identify them, we can change the outcome, and change our lives, not just move forward despite the perceived *dysfunction*.

Don't shortchange your findings, for even when we've discovered the problem, the root still needs to be exposed.

As you go through this book you will find the top 3 of 10 responses from women when asked about what they wished they had received from their fathers. I've added 3 chapters as precursors to help us gain greater understanding of how the construct and topic can affect our outlook and interactions.

A word of wisdom, read on with the knowing that everyone is not perfect but remember the good that you have received and how whatever you've experienced has benefited you, being cautious not to focus on the bad.

A word of instruction, it can be tempting to skip the topical reflection chapters, however, please do not move ahead. Chapter 1 and 2 sets a foundation for what we'll be exploring. Chapter 3 and 4 discusses identity and daughterhood and what they mean for us. Chapter 5 starts the impactive topics.

Introduction

The general set up of the chapters are as follows; First, I will give general definitions, then share with you my interpretations of them. After, I may share a personal story, and then dive into how I believe each experience affect our being.

You will also have the opportunity to reflect and express your feelings by writing them out. I suggest you have a notebook or a journal handy for this as the allotted space may not be enough for you to express your thoughts and feeling.

At this point, I will note that I am aware that substitutions are sometimes provided that fill possible void. When you're getting all you need to fulfill, you don't sense a need for anything else. There seems to be no lack, no void, no curiosity about your shaping and molding into the whole you, or why you didn't receive what others did.

I believe that all our paths, and journeys along them are different, even when there are many similarities. While you may not be able to personally identify with all the content, perhaps you may grab pieces that make sense to you, and if nothing else, more than anything else, help someone else.

I also caution against skipping over the written process. Harbored unhealthy thoughts and feelings is to your disadvantage. They cause stress and sickness and keep us captive in its grip. Writing out your revelations and feelings can offer a level of release of tension, burden and pain. Get it out! Or at least, write it!

I will share truths that will enlighten, words that give direction, and while you may experience a cut here or there, you will sustain. It is simple and to the point. My prayer is that through it, we can morph, and walk in the fullness given us from the beginning of time.

Whether we realize the depth of it or not, or even care to admit it, you are a ***reflection of your father.***

With that, let's journey to understand us, and others like us, to be a better us, to a better you, a better daughter, sister, friend, mother. Woman.

I hope it enlightens, confirms and blesses you as much as it has me writing it.

Let "Us" begin!

CHAPTER 1

Reflection

A reflection is more than what you recognize casting back at you by a body or surface of light. As in a mirror, the reflection reveals the image that is before it, allowing you to see more of yourself; the part of you that you rarely look at, until you either intently or are forced to stand before it.

When you do, you not only observe the image in front of it, but you're capable of seeing more of what's behind you without turning back. But it primarily provides you with the chance to take a more intent look at yourself, to examine the you, you rarely take time to explore.

The mirror captures what's in its background, but it doesn't give names, identify its objects, or discern the importance of what's before it. It only reveals the picture being reflected.

A Reflection of my Father expresses that very sentiment. When looking in the mirror, everything you are is being reflected. Though you can't see them directly, all of your diverse experiences, your beliefs, your decisions you've made; and in this case, all that has been deposited into you by your father, what you've gained or may have missed due to lack of his influence is being revealed before you, even when you can't perceive it. You have to dig deep and search wide to find the you that's burrowed behind your years of experiences.

When I gained the courage to stand before it, the mirror presented to me an image I accepted because of what *I* chose to believe about myself, and the decisions I've made as a result of what I chose to believe. It forced me to investigate those hidden places and exposed areas that no one else had seen.

A Reflection of My Father articulates how my father impacted my life in many areas, even though I didn't discern it until my adult years. From infantry through adulthood, we intrinsically seek comfort, peace, trust, and confirmation. What we neglect is to understand the place for the masculine voice, and the strength it commits or fail to give. His voice is a springboard for many things we allow ourselves to accept and endure, and these things have impacted your decisions, and the person you see is the product of them.

These decisions are based on how we've interpreted our past, how we predict our future based on hope, how we regard ourselves, the way we present ourselves, and the way we interact with others. Our decisions directly position us for what our next looks like.

Reflection

Our next not only involves us but affects others. In every way (since adulthood) we've had the choice to construct our lives how we desire it to be. Whether that choice was for our good or created some drawbacks, they were ours.

We may not quite have understood why we've made certain decisions when it comes to relationships and love. I propose it's closely connected to our relationship with our fathers during our childhood and our adult life that continues to transmit our joys, comforts, fears, and disdain.

When we make adult decisions based on our little girl experiences, we delay healing and enlightenment, and we prolong the feelings of disappointment and heartache. Affected by our pinned-up frustrations, we allow them to influence or even govern our decisions, sometimes without us realizing it.

Therewith, when we continually **allow** others to disappoint and hurt us, we commit self-betrayal. We disregard our own truths, sacrifice our own hearts, and drain every ounce of energy we've mustered up to make others happy, or at least, satisfied.

It seems and feels like a perpetual cycle of expending ourselves. Until it does end. When we've had enough of pouring out of ourselves with little reciprocation, there needs to be a turning point. One that alters our life's trajectory. If not, we will stay in a cycle of bondage.

Years ago I realized that *it is foolish to continue to build on a porous foundation. It can be easily cracked, broken and crumble and you'll find yourself sinking underneath the rubble.* We must shine a light on the vulnerable, tainted areas of our hearts and minds. Light gives darkness no place to hide and reveals the truth, tear down lies, and you, the person, can be restored and rebuilt.

When you are aware of what's real, and the difference between the fruit of authenticity and the byproduct of deception (the lies that you are bombarded with daily), understanding is at the door awaiting entry. You can then establish on the truth.

The Mirror

When you look in the mirror what do you see? Who do you see? Look past the aesthetic nature, to the innermost parts of your being. The very depths of your soul want to be found, to be known, to emerge. I encourage you, even more, I implore you, to see beyond the temporal exteriors and explore. Peel back the layers and breathe in every part of you.

For many, it is an unpleasant task. Axiomatically, this task can be simple, while the simplicity of this act can be quite complex. The façades we choose to wear each day become the *who* we begin to identify with, and it can stand in the way of the authentic you.

These facades may reveal a small component of who we are, partially express who we want to be, or how we desire to be viewed. However, facades only offer a superficial and deceptive view, and in no way define our true selves, yet we give them autonomy and permission for them to speak on our behalf.

They portray to the world we are what we're not, and we're not what we are. They'll rob us of joy, our truth, our identity. Façades can display a picture of joy and happiness, when we're filled with doubt and fear, contemplating our own detriment. It will scream wealth and health when we're facing distressing battles. Others presume a position of anger and hate when its only sadness lurking. Some are even beguiled into believing the façade of confidence when insecurity is the prominent state of mind. They can become so tangible to us that we even begin to believe them ourselves.

> *Facades may reveal a small component of who we are, but facades only offer a superficial and deceptive view, yet we give them autonomy and permission for them to speak on our behalf.*

But when we're alone, our realities remind us that there is something unreal, unnatural. This reality convinces us to be able to reveal glimpses of ourselves to the very few who see beyond the internal and external deception.

Defining self is a task that we dare to dive into, but that is precisely our goal. It means looking further and deeper into places fear and denial has prevented you from uncovering. To know who we are, we should learn and attempt to understand the place from which we came–revealing history, sometimes even to generations. But I want to make this a little simpler, and immediate. Let's look at where we are directly impacted by one who shares our DNA, and is a direct expression of you, your father.

Some believe that your fathers' DNA is the most dominant in their expression. While my goal is not to prove it, we know his gene determines your sex. This, in no way, discredits the part a mother has, both of them are equally important and add distinct qualities to their child's life. These ideas simply aid in my claim that, you *are* a reflection of your father.

It is because of my own relationship with my father that I am influenced to write this. I believe they have a vital role in our lives. While I possess many of my mother's character traits, my fathers' impact on my life has been immense.

His words of encouragement I hold dear, and they often ring through my mind. As I hear his voice telling me, *I can and I will*, I vividly see his smile.

I remember how secure I felt when he hugged me. He made me feel like I was the most beautiful person, the most intelligent and the most loved girl in the world.

When searching for your place, you ask the questions in some form, who am I? Where do I belong? What is my purpose? I believe that what our fathers can pour into us helps direct those answers. It bears the weight that speaks to your heart mind and soul. In his

Reflection

presence, or in his absence, is the potential to both fill us or cause us to feel a void.

Even as our childhood realities reveal themselves in adulthood, any abuses we have experienced can be overcome.

This can be the start of your new beginning in your new-found truth-your renewed identity. This is the time for you to release what hold you back and grow forward!

A Reflection of My Father

Reflections of Reflection

This reflection calls for action.

Rise up the moment you are reading this.
Now take a deep breath.
Exhale.
Make your way to the nearest mirror where you can clearly see your whole bare face.
If you are dressed in make-up, remove it.
Take a deep breath.
Exhale.
Now, look.
Look at yourself.
Look at your face.
Your eyes.
Your brows.
Your lashes.
The color of your eyes.
Your nose, your ears, your cheekbones.
Your chin.
Your lips.
Your mouth.
Your smile.
Your forehead.
Your head, your hair, even
Your neck.
Look at the lines, the length of it. The width of it.

Reflection

1. What are your thoughts?

   _____
   _____
   _____
   _____
   _____
   _____
   _____

2. How do you *feel* when you look at yourself in the mirror?

   _____
   _____
   _____
   _____
   _____
   _____
   _____

> Now look again. Look deep into your eyes
> for at least 3 minutes.

3. What are you experiencing?

_____

_____

_____

_____

_____

_____

_____

4. What do you struggle looking at?

_____

_____

_____

_____

_____

_____

_____

5. Why?

_____

_____

_____

_____

_____

_____

_____

It will get easier.

CHAPTER 2

My Life, My Story

Your story is a term you'll hear often in scholastic and professional settings. Your story informs people of who you are, your background, what you do, etc. But in order to even tell your story you have to know it.

I believe we should think about who we are, your reason for being and what encouraged you to be where you are. The story usually helps others to understand a bit of your history or motivation whether its immediate history or distant.

In the context of this book, I want to share a portion of my story. The part about how I wanted to be seen perfect in my dad's eyes. I wish I had been the perfect girl for him, and if I had known better, I would've gleaned much more from him than I allowed myself to.

Perhaps in my naivety, I felt my father would be here forever, so I would have all the time in the world with him. He was a super-hero, not only mine but for many others as well. Our lives were jolted with a sad reality in 1995 when we lost him.

How does a super-hero leave so soon, and what will I do now? The voice that gave me so much hope, inspiration, and so much love, I wouldn't hear anymore. No matter what anyone would try to say to comfort me; he's still with you in your heart; you have your memories, yadda, yadda, yadda, gibberish is what it sounded like, and none of it would bring peace in this new reality.

Memories are not the same as hearing his voice, his wet sloppy kisses on my face, his embrace, and even getting disciplined with two-fingers to the top of my forehead. Being in his presence or even the anticipation of it, was soothing and brought unspeakable joy to my heart.

Memories are not the same, but I hold on to them, gripping them as tightly as I wish I'd held onto him. His laughter and gentleness spoke volumes about his character and love. I remember how he protected and provided for us to the best of his ability, his discipline was an extension of that love and concern. I remember how his acceptance and his presence made all the difference. Even now, his influence on my life continues to be revealed, and it continues to refine me. These memories have become as priceless as the jewel he made me to believe I was. No, they are not the same, but they are all I have.

I loved my father beyond words! Our relationship was filled with adoration, respect, favor and love. I, in my own mind, was the apple of his eye, but my sisters may argue the same. Words alone cannot express how I view our relationship, and yet, when I look back, I still see areas for improvement.

Many people would probably agree that if they were younger, they would have made some changes. In fact, very few people would think otherwise. But as the saying goes, hindsight is 20/20 (or for clearer sight, 20/10), but forth sight is enhanced by wisdom and experience. We can learn to make wiser decisions the more we give attention to important aspects of a relationship with others and self.

I've made many mistakes, had misconceptions and missed opportunities to step into who I was. I've often thought, if only I had taken a different approach, made different decisions, or seized those opportunities, things would be very different. On the other hand, if I had found a different way, made different choices or taken other chances, I may not have been who I am today.

The woman I've come to love and appreciate would be different. I may not be living the life I am now, nor would I be writing this book, with this content, or with the same perspective.

As I continue to share a portion of my story, my prayer is to help you begin to understand that no matter how perfect things seem to be, there are lessons, disappointments, shortcomings, challenges to overcome, and weaknesses that need to be strengthened.

I hope to help you recognize how my experiences and personal relationship with my father help set the pace for my interactions in my future relationships. How I, as a young lady, unconsciously accepted behaviors that were contrary to what I had been shown due to my interpretations of my relationship with my father and how I erroneously applied them to my then current experience.

Due to my ignorance and naivety, I gained a false sense of strength and security, resulting in me not being true to myself. I bequeathed my power as a human being, and my worth as a young lady. However, I also want you to know that it was that same state of naivety that helped me endure some rough times, recover, forgive, and heal as well. The point to this is that no matter what you experience, how you interpret those experiences, how you respond to them, how you use them to strengthen and grow; they are used as a steppingstone to your greatness. As long as you keep moving, keep pushing and keep standing, if you don't give up, things will work for you.

My daddy was an awesome man. He was intelligent (genius-like in my book), funny (kind of a corny funny) and brought me so much joy; my knight in shining armor so to speak. I absolutely adored him.

While I always saw him as the perfect dad, he was not a perfect infallible man, no one is. At least, that's what I came to understand as I matured.

He was human, which meant he made mistakes. He was human, so he couldn't be everywhere all the time even if we wanted him to be. He was human, so he wasn't all-knowing, no matter how smart and intelligent he was. He was human, so he couldn't provide and fulfill my every need, desire or dream although he may've mostly tried.

My parents divorced when my brother and I were toddlers, and my mother moved to a city about 2 ½ hours away. We were back and forth for years alternating summers and school seasons between parents. I became used to the routine. In fact, I looked forward to it! Time with mom was cool, but since I was daddy's little girl, for a long while that's where I wanted to be most.

My dad worked a lot, helping support three sets of children, 1 from a previous marriage prior to my mom, my brother and myself and his then current family. It wasn't an easy task I'm sure, but it's what he needed to do.

When he was home he was often resting because of the long hours. Even though I coveted more time with him, I was mostly ok with just being at my second home, even when he wasn't there. I knew why he had to be gone a lot. He was building and providing for his family. I know that relationships aren't always just about being physically available and to build you may have to sacrifice, so I excused his temporary absence in my mind, despite my longing for his attention and his presence.

I was pretty much the middle child. My siblings were either older, too old for me to hang with, and I thought the same about my younger siblings, I was too old for them to hang with me. My brothers that were closer to my age had their own friends, and they were boys, so their younger sister couldn't really hang out with them. So I had to learn to enjoy life as a child by myself, and then with my friends.

As I grew, I recognized how my ability to adapt to our family circumstances, and the long distance and hours had affected me. In fact, my ability to adapt either created an inability to recognize when there was imbalance, or as before, just put the behavior out of my mind.

With my father, I was too young to know that the distance that became normal wasn't just in the miles we traveled. I didn't realize until later during my dating years that I would be so used to "distance" that I accepted degrees of separation in my relationships, with whom I was dating and with friends. So the distance that became so normal continued.

I was living my own life. I was self-sufficient and self-fulfilling, independent, and mostly confident. I had me, my family and my girls. If I had a boyfriend, he didn't have to be around a lot, and I wasn't concerned with what he was doing. He could pretty much do what he wanted considering I was preoccupied with my life. That included him being MIA for a time. If he only came by or called once to a few times a week, that was fine, as long as he was consistent in that. The arrangement was easy and worked for me.

Then I began to feel like there should be more contact, and the distance was no longer acceptable to me. The problem was, he wasn't there, and we weren't building, anything.

My father showed me love and support, regardless of his flaws. I believed his love and counted on his strength. He was my encourager and my strength. His love made me look past his flaws, even unrecognizing them, and his love shined through. His love for me made me love him more.

My father would make sure I was well taken care of no matter what he had to do. My daddy would always be there to love and protect me. And with him, his absence was forgivable because he was, well, my dad.

Later in life I saw the same scenario under different circumstances. Daddy had prepared me for things I didn't see coming, or that seemed non-threatening to my future. He had softened my heart to a man that was doing what he "had to." I had learned to inconvenience my heart without expressing my disdain, and my behavior became that of compliance and disregard of myself, all while thinking I was good, and I didn't need a lot in my relationships.

The truth was that I had trained him how to treat me. That it took little effort to appease or satisfy me, until the next time we saw each other.

As I became more aware of betrayal and being devalued, I pushed myself to step outside of my circumstance to see what I was missing. I had to learn the difference in a low-maintenance relationship and a disrespectful, unfulfilling one. Not just disrespectful in ways that were obvious, but in ways that can escape your attention if you're not looking, or if you turn away enough.

It became quite clear to me that I wanted more than what I was experiencing. I desired change. I had had enough. Enough of being tolerated. Enough of actually feeling deserted. Enough of waiting for him to be, ready. Enough of settling for just enough.

The Outlook

You can look at other people and never know or understand what they've experienced. If we're honest with ourselves, we've all dealt with things we feel we shouldn't have, been treated in ways we didn't deserve, or maybe even settled in areas we shouldn't have.

When it comes to relationships, projects, or endeavors, your goal is to see ripe fruit or a reasonable return. So if you're going to commit yourself to something or someone, that object of commitment needs to be worth it or at least reciprocal. Otherwise, we are going through the same process of expending and bequeathing of your energy, time and power.

While my life didn't seem that bad in the moments, anything outside of true commitment was an injustice to me as a woman and as a human being. When a relationship demands you to accept a betrayal of self, it's not worth the time, energy or your heart.

I had shortchanged love and commitment and accepted temporary gratification as their replacement. I certainly wanted commitment, honesty, loyalty and intimacy, but pride and a false sense of security and strength stood in the way. I was blinded by temporary fixes of lust and admiration, and for a long time I didn't even realize that love and commitment was what I was missing. In fact, I didn't even know that they were necessary for a healthy and fulfilling relationship.

Perhaps I didn't even know that I should want them. I hadn't consciously considered it much before then, but my heart had felt it all along. When you're lacking something, you tend to try to build yourself up to create a sense of completion where a void has occurred, so you don't feel the effects of the intrusion of displacements.

I know my father had to work to take care of family even if it meant being away for long periods of time. He had 10 children! He didn't stay away because he thought he was cool or was too busy sowing his oats. He was gone because at that time, he had to be.

My father was tired, but with the decisions he made as a young man, he had to step up. Sacrifices had to be made to help meet our needs. Unfortunately, time with

A Reflection of My Father

us was one of those sacrifices. That time missed took valuable lessons along with it.

Regardless, I knew his love for us was immeasurable. It was because he loved that he did what he had to do although, his love couldn't be measured by what he did. Love was his motivation; provision was his responsibility.

Still, he found time somewhere in between work and sleep to make us smile and belch out a laugh, to tell corny jokes (I would have never told him that.). take us to the show, jut town or to the carnival, and most importantly, he made the time to say I love you, kiss our faces and hug us up.

As I matured, I began to see myself; who I was, what I wanted and what I was no longer willing to accept. My boundaries became clearer and clearer. I learned the expectations I had for relationships didn't match my heart's desire.

I learned that I certainly wanted to be loved. Love treated me kind and warmed my heart. Love wanted to be near (even if I felt I wanted to disappear from its presence at times). Love accepted and appreciated me, all of me, my laughs, in fact love made me laugh, it acknowledged my cries to comfort me, exposed my flaws to develop me, celebrated my beauty, welcomed my intelligence, delighted in my corniness, empowered my uniqueness, spoke to my failures with encouragement, challenged my views to sharpen me and questioned my motives to bring awareness and maturity.

Love covered my wrongs with forgiveness and graced my unyielding nature with patience. Love accepted me, the good and the not so good. This is what I learned from my father. Yes, my dad had also taught me that.

Anything that speaks differently would welcome brokenness. I discovered that love wasn't something I longed for; it was something I knew.

And while my daddy wasn't always there, he was always available. At any moment I could awaken him and tap into the wisdom, experience his affection and enjoy his humor.

He would validate me in my weakness, doubts and fears. He would make me feel strong, safe and enough. And he clothed me in love. I wasn't longing for something I wasn't familiar with; we had been slightly estranged, but I knew love. I'd had it all my life.

See, what I learned, is that a father need not just be physically present, he need not always validate as we think he should, he need not express love the way we think we deserve. His greatest obligation as a father is to only put forth his best.

Know that his best may not be your idea of best. When he does all he knows how and it's still not everything you think you need, when you feel like you didn't get enough love, enough validation, enough time, and you always feel like you're still missing something, think of the best of who you are. His best or worst foot forward may have been the drive, the force that pushed

A Reflection of My Father

you to do better and be the best you, you know how in your moments.

That is what the reflection shows. It is the image you mirror. The love and the rejection, the time and the absence, the validation or the ridicule. That reflection is what kept you going, kept you pushing, kept you moving.

It's not the answer to the questions, but the questions themselves that leads you down the path to finding your truth, but the expectations of the answers pull you in.

Often, when the path is faced with challenges, to the mind, body or spirit, we stop and fail to move pass the process of identification. But moving forward means digging deeper and identifying the source of inner turmoil.

Here is a nugget for your notebook;

In any relationship we can find ourselves reacting to things in unseemly ways. Ways you couldn't have possibly imagined in any situation. When we're confronted with things that touch our emotions or even punch us in the gut, we can either have no response, just an internal response, a developed one or and unpredictable one.

Internalizing can make you sick, don't do it. If you need to process in that way, okay, but at some time you must share what you feel with the right person. That would be the one who made you feel that way and someone else you can trust to be the voice of reason and wisdom.

Unpredictable responses can send you on a path of the unpredictable. No one knows how you will act, including you. It is an unsafe path that you do not want to embark. Unpredictable means uncontrolled and uncontrol can get you into a lot of trouble.

No response can usually mean you are so used to what you're dealing with. It is no surprise, so you go about your day as usual. This is an ingredient for a sour batch. You can already be bitter or sick, choosing not to deal with an injustice because it's just not worth a response, and you still stay in the relationship, intimate or otherwise. Or you could be tired of hearing the same untruths and you're planning an escape. If so, then hurray for you!

A developed response delivers wisdom. You refused to deal with non-sense, or you've dealt with it so long that you've had enough.

Before I veer off into a completely different topic, let's see how this is connected to what I'm writing about.

The term daddy issues, or issues with your father didn't rise out of the land of nod. It originated to help identify the something beyond the surface that pushes our pain, insecurities, discomforts and fears. The what that causes us to repeat the cycles of pain without pinpointing why until you go through a process of discovery.

All our stories aren't pretty. All our heartbreaks aren't because our parents felt our suitors were unworthy. Our experiences go deeper. Our hearts, tenderness, feelings, humility, our womanhood, is buried in heaps of coal brooding a fire underneath the surface needing to breathe. The brilliant gems are waiting to be revealed, if it can withstand the flames.

Let's dig way down deep to uproot the harmful, hurtful and unfruitful habits and actions.

My Life, My Story

Reflections of My Life, Your Story

1. What is your story? What was/is your relationship with your father?

   _____
   _____
   _____
   _____
   _____
   _____

2. How did the relationship make you feel growing up?

   _____
   _____
   _____
   _____
   _____
   _____

3. How do you feel about the relationship now?

   _____
   _____
   _____
   _____
   _____
   _____
   _____

A Reflection of My Father

4. Attempt to put away any feelings of anger if you have them right now. Those feeling will result in answer like, who cares?, I don't care. It doesn't matter one way or the other, or similar responses.

   In what way did your relationship with your father affect or impacted you the most?

   _____
   _____
   _____
   _____
   _____
   _____
   _____
   _____
   _____

5. Is there anything you feel you've missed or needed in your life that wasn't given to you? If yes, what is it?

   _____
   _____
   _____
   _____
   _____
   _____
   _____
   _____
   _____
   _____

6. What things did you give up or hand over because you didn't understand that it was precious and valuable?

_____
_____
_____
_____
_____
_____
_____
_____
_____

7. How and when did you give your power away?

_____
_____
_____
_____
_____
_____
_____
_____
_____

You can get it back.

CHAPTER 3

Identity

What's in a Name

***B**eautiful flower.* According to daddy, that's what my name meant. Each time I'd ask, he gave an arching grin, and his reply was aphoristic, *Beautiful flower* because of course, flowers are beautiful, right? That flower was me. That's what he thought of me and that's what I believed.

As I'm writing this, It's dawning on me that I've known the importance of identity since I was a little girl. I had been asking what my name meant since I could remember as if I understood that it somehow helped me identify with who I was.

My father named me. He had insight from the beginning (after my mom denied him the rights to name me Cecil, ha-ha). Beautiful flower would combat any negative words spoken against my natural beauty, aesthetically and intrinsically. It was a gesture that suggested the beauty of my nature to the heart of me.

I remember as a teenager; one of my sister's friend told me that I was so cute, then added the words, *all the way up to here*, and made a gesture that stopped before my smile.

> *If we don't change the tandem of negative words, they can become a hindrance to our growth.*

I thought she was a very pretty girl. Being about 7 years my senior at the time and my sisters' best friend, I respected and valued what she said.

But the moment she spoke those words, I began to dismiss her in my heart because it didn't feel right to me. It was at that moment I realized that she didn't really like me, and she was trying to hurt me. Because of the respect I had for her as a little girl, I remember her words, even still.

I think about how words stick with us throughout our years, positive and negative. Good positive encouraging words build us up and help us flourish. Negative words tear us down. If we don't change its tandem early on they can stay with us for a lifetime. We think about them as they are embedded in our conscious and subconscious and we can come to believe their lie. They possibly will become a hindrance to our growth.

I've had many compliments on my smile throughout the years. Being told that it was beautiful, amazing, it was an asset, that it brightened others day, etc. But I'll never forget those words during my fragile years.

It's not that I believe them now, but they influenced me. At times, I've questioned the brightness of my smile, but I remind myself of the *beautiful flower* I am. I look in the mirror and see the smile that brightens my day–the smile that I love.

In my mid to late-20's, while at a meeting, I met an older woman on an elevator. She was elated when she read my name tag. *Shaia!!* She said. *My name is Shaia!* She informed me that it was a Hebrew name. *Blessed. It means blessed.* I gave her the biggest smile to show I shared her enthusiasm, then thanked her.

Well, that explains it. The reason why I have this joy, this favor over my life, and able to show love for others no matter the challenges I face. Blessed, yes, that sums it up.

Later in my years, further research revealed that the extended meaning of my name truly defined my nature. I am, one who flies above the clouds, as an eagle. No matter what I endure, I will always rise and fly above the storms of life. Your perspective is different when your position is changed. From an aerial view, I can fly high, look low, and soar.

While your name is not what completely identifies you, I believe it is a large part of your expression, your character. Your name is attached to you and defines the integrity of your nature, and what people call you is what they're constantly speaking over you.

My name is *Shaia*. Blessed. One who soars above the clouds. Shaia, Shaia, Shaia, blessed, blessed, blessed, soar, soar, soar. See, people have been calling me blessed, and telling me to soar all my life! I love my name! Call Me Shaia. Hold the nicknames; those are reserved for my hubby, family and close friends.

You must insist on your right to be called by your name. If you allow others to call you out of your name, you are allowing your right to the manifestation of your identity to be stripped from you. If you allow others to curse your name, or replace your name with a curse, you are, in a sense, renouncing your identity, and agreeing to the reversal of the blessing that is, by right, yours to be spoken over you each day of your life. It can interfere with who you are to morph into along different stages of your journey.

This same effect happens when you are completely unaware of who you are or what your name means. There can be many hiccups that you find yourself in, and you may be unmotivated to get pass. Knowing the gift of what has been assigned to you (your name), reveals what you are connected to, and at times can give you the motivation to keep moving.

Now that I know I am connected to and am a product of blessings, and I understand what blessed means, I will expect that in every circumstance and every area of my life, I will walk in blessings and I expect nothing less.

Identity

Your name is the representation of you. And if you don't agree with it, change it!

Shaping My Existence

It seems almost needless to say that many people today have struggled with their identity at some point, yet, it's necessary to remind you that many people are challenged daily with thoughts of significance.

Even those that may appear the most confident, question who they are and the validity to stand against either the person next to them or their previous successes.

Since childhood we've been curious about other people, and in relation to our own position, where they stood.

We ask their names, to identify them, then wonder why their distinguishing features are different from our own. Why do I, or they look different, or why their hair, nose, ears, eyes, skin is different? You get it right?

These questions enter our minds at an early age. Sometimes subtle, and other times it resembles the invasion of the 50th kind.

We are constantly fighting to be what our mind's eye is telling us we should. In other words, what you're constantly seeing or watching (giving attention to) is becoming a planted image we either with the conscience or subconscious, work to become like. Adopting and adapting to the accepted.

From the moment we meet life outside of the womb we are being shaped. Everything from our community to home environment, to our inner circles, begin to shape us. With so many having a hand in whom we're to become, it's no wonder why there are so many questions about our purpose.

Without a sure and sound foundation of our who and our why, our identity is an experience away from being stripped, and we are left questioning our very existence.

I've seen parents attempt to mold their children into mini versions of themselves. In doing so the child's individuality is overlooked and dishonored. When parents have missed their own opportunities to pursue their true passion, their desire can get pushed on their children. Parents, from their children's early years even into adulthood, program their children to believe their passion is identical to their own. In the main interest of themselves, their push and personal desire, parents can miss opportunities to draw out the gifts that usher their child to their threshold of destiny. This is why there are so many being pushed into sports, entertainment, and other careers that we find ourselves unhappy? It is predominantly done for their parents.

This doesn't mean that success isn't found in these areas; we see that it does every day. Yet, while these successes open the door to many opportunities for them, they have also allowed happiness, joy, peace and other things so greatly desired, to slip through their fingers.

Identity

Even when we believe we are making our own decisions, program kicks in. We find ourselves doing the things we were taught or trained to do, whether it is for our good, or disagreeable to integrity, character, or our future, the influences of your life tend to speak louder than your own voice, mostly because we don't recognize our own voice.

A parent's true intention is and should be for their children to have more and to do better than *they* did. The line gets crossed when we fail to take the time to get to know our children. Having conversations that are meaningful and cater to them in ways that will allow them to express their own desires and hopes.

Giving advice or sharing your own experiences are beneficial to a daughter's development, and it gives them different outlooks and direction but forcing her or them to pursue only what *you* think is best, can cause them to become compliant to not only your demands and expectations, but other men who are in more dominant positions. A daughter holds on to her fathers' every word and that word, if you're not cautious, will drive her to clench her own purpose before she even truly discovers it.

If a father bombards his daughter with *his* vision, he forces her to decide between following his plan or discovering her own (something she wishes he would guide her in instead).

There is a lot to live up to if we leave it up to others. The world attempts to compel us to deny our own identities, to resemble its idea of beauty, normality and womanhood. We can get lost in a pigeon's nest and struggle to clear any blurred lines between *who you are,* and *who you were convinced to believe you were.*

To avoid the worlds enthrallment and a tumultuous influx of unrealistic expectations, we must be able to define our roles; in relationships, society, work environment and in any given circumstance.

Knowing your position helps you manage your life so you can operate in the place that has already been prepared for you to move and excel in, and if at any time you happen to veer off that path, it is more easily recognizable.

Understanding your position means that you are less likely to give of yourself beyond what you are humanly required (required, as in operating in the law of *giving* and receiving, and outside of selfishness).

Here we can also begin to examine the idea of implicit individual acculturation by recognizing areas where we've been shaped through popular and pervasive dominance of society, in boldness and subtleties, both consciously and subconsciously. In other words, we can weigh the scales in those areas where we are convinced by others to conform to popular views and beliefs.

As you embark on a journey of self, you become acutely aware of the you that was once hidden behind misunderstanding, miscommunication, confusion, pain, and even laughter, happiness, pursuits of grander and comfortability.

You'll experience sweet surprises and have bitter memories that will regulate your outlook on life. Setting your face for continual self-examination against the truth of your identity opens you up to focus on the deeper aspects of yourself, not the criticism of man.

Entanglements with difficult people and situations continues to teach us how to manage relationships better and set boundaries so personal space is understood and respected.

We can change and move forward with joy, peace of mind and a deeper appreciation for the gift of your life, without repeating the same deafening, stabilizing, illusive cycles.

In my journey, I began to recognize behaviors that hindered my own growth. Acknowledgment of them allowed me to create new behaviors that enhanced my character and laid along my path many opportunities for personal development. So when I look back, I would see the who I was, the changes I've made to be who I am now and accept and love the me that's on the potters' wheel, being molded into the most unique and wonderful graceful pillar.

Face to Face

Your perspective of yourself is who you will eventually become, because what you choose to identify with influences your decisions, and those decisions shape your existence. You begin to act on what *you* view as the truth of your identity. Every action and each decision you make shapes your future. You ultimately, regardless of the actions of others, have determined the trajectory of your life.

You will get to the place where you'll have to come face to face with *yourself*. Things you didn't, or felt you didn't have a choice in before has now become your chance to decide whether you'll allow your greatness to flow. You must find your strengths, embrace fearlessness and decide what you choose to identify with.

I have chosen to identify with one who has the dexterity and assurance to exceed at anything she chooses.

I identify with being endowed with favor.

I identify with the eagle which takes full flight, soaring above the clouds with an aerial view.

I identify with resiliency.

I identify with being beautiful. A beautiful, flower.

I Am, who my father seeded, and whom my mother bore. I Am Me, the beautiful flower that is essential, exceeds, excels, endures, embodies greatness, and extraordinary! I am blessed!

Merriam dictionary defines *identity* as:

Sameness of essential or generic character in different instances

b : sameness in all that constitutes the objective reality of a thing**:** ONENESS

Identity

This description is what I'm referring to because it is in this context where the general makeup of our identity is understood.

My father was a part of several organizations that were essential to our local communities. Whether he ever considered it to be a part of his identity, I don't believe, but what I do know is that even though he was a part of them, he was not disconnected from himself.

He found the time to listen to the music he enjoyed and watching the news. He made some time to spend with his children, in addition to being a husband and so many things to other people.

Fathers help us gain a perspective of individuality while being a part of something more than ourselves. How do you not lose yourself while fitting into something greater?

Individuality I understood, but I had to learn boundaries. When I take on something I like to give it my all, but I would often find myself trying to give it more than I could actually spare; my heart, mind and my time. I needed to learn the boundaries between the individual me, and the me that was a part of something else, something greater, without losing myself to it. This is a steady charge because my considerable personality wants to continue in the habit, but it's less daunting than before.

Every day we are pushed to the boundary line of decision. Time with my father and our circumstances showed me that I can do whatever I wanted while being me, but it didn't allow for teaching and giving me direction on how to identify my role in this big space. Those are things I had to discover on my own. And I had to learn to make decisions that were best for my well-being in any space.

Face to face takes us back to the reflection in the mirror. It causes us to look at the present, and for but a moment, remember the past to reveal the distance we've traveled and the lessons we've learned and help develop an encouraging outlook of our future.

It gives you the chance to face the fears, imperfections, blemishes, the bruises and celebrate the beauty that lies beneath, waiting to be revealed.

As we go through life's stages, we should experience change and have evolved from who we were even just five years ago, and you should essentially recognize that growth. Going through the self-discovery process we often uncover valuable lessons we missed and realize that we've embraced many ideas, habits, and lifestyles because it made sense to who we were at that moment. We've settled into whatever state we decided to adjust to and whatever level of comfort or discomfort we've mentally agreed therefore, find ourselves doing the same things we were years ago, even if we no longer agree to or like them. So it is revealed, our habits, influence or lifestyle didn't change much at all.

Just as you'll find that how you received as a young girl and how you process may be different now, but there is still the possibility that the capacity to receive what was lacking may be quite similar to how it was those many years ago. This is because while you may have grown and matured in many areas, things we weren't given in our childhood haven't been watered and nurtured, therefore there's still need for growth and development in those areas.

And while a change needs to happen, we often prolong it because change doesn't seem easy or comfortable. Someone so elegantly adjudicated that people are resistant to change themselves.

This happens for more than one reason.

Stanley Hauerwas, in Hannah's Child: A Theologian's Memoir stated;

"When you are trying to change the questions, you have to realize that many people are quite resistant to such a change. They like the answers they have."

People want to stay in *their* comfortable place. It takes work, physically and mentally to change habits, decisions, and lifestyle, while managing the emotions behind them. It can be a task making what seems to be drastic changes, but when you start, you'll find it isn't as difficult as we made ourselves believe.

Another reason is that sometimes people aren't aware that change needs to happen. They don't stay where they are because they don't want to change, they stay where they are because they don't know that they *need to* change, and the things that are for their benefit are brushed off because of the unawareness of its' necessity.

Sometimes, others will see you before you see yourself. There is something my husband always say that drives this thought forward, *you should at least consider a viewpoint before you immediately deny it*. I mention this to say, don't dismiss the experiences or insights shared and pass them off as "other peoples' issues." If we consider the "read" or the callout, it could quite possibly be enlightening and challenge your mind to revelation.

Face to Face–Deciding to change means you are open to growing, evolving to a better you. You determine how you'll approach the process, but keep in mind that self-discovery is ongoing. Remember to stay open to who you are now, who you are becoming and who you could become.

While going through the process, remember the little girl. Allow her to come out. Don't drown her out. Talk to her. Let her face her fears, face her challenges, face her mishaps, face her disappointments. Listen to her, identify with her, empathize with her, cry with her, laugh with her and embrace her.

Things will begin to unfold; you will begin to understand and can come to grips with why you may have certain challenges and struggle in areas and why you are so successful in others.

If you openly embrace the image that stands before the mirror, continue to behold, self-discovery will be like opening a gift on a big day. If you're expecting something great, what you find inside will meet your

Identity

anticipation. If you don't expect much or anything at all, what's inside should exceed your expectations.

Your perception of it is everything. Your perception truly helps determine what your next steps and what your future will be. Continual self-discoveries compel more self-examinations. See, no matter how exciting or painful what you find, see yourself getting closer to a release of burdens and breaking of chains, and see yourself getting that much closer to healing and freedom.

There is a certain power in coming face to face with self. But with each phase of it, you not only learn more about who you are but more about who you have the potential to be, walking as a whole person. Keeping in mind that none are perfect, not one of us, but we all can strive to be better and become the perfect us.

Our experiences bring growth or stagnation; you choose which. Be clear with your boundaries. Do so by gaining a better understanding of who you are. It's a very challenging feat to do and be when you don't know who that person is.

The biggest downfall with not knowing who you are is that if you don't know or aren't comfortable with who you are, anyone can persuade you to be who and what they want you to be.

My parents poured this into me since the day they named me. Identity makes you feel like you have something to connect to, like you're a part of something and it helps give some kind of assurance. I am assured that I am blessed.

We have learned to grow in our current roles but many of us have also abandoned the privileges of being a daughter and it is a great injustice to all when we abandon daughterhood.

Okay Being Me

Other people's perspectives on what they see are certainly not always the same as what I know to be true. At times, I see fairness, while others may see beauty, and yet others may see an unpleasantry in my aesthetics, but who really cares? Even in my fairness, I am still beautiful. If no one else sees it, "it's still well with me, and if everyone does, it won't move me.

I've learned to embrace my beauty, my quirks, and imperfections, and those things I don't love, I appreciate and accept it for what it is, a part of me. However, I am cautious not to offend others with the awareness of my own identity.

Understand that our flaws revealed doesn't make us weak or pitiful. If we acknowledge them, we are vulnerable only to strength. If we're intentional, we change, we grow, we evolve, and we encourage others to explore, despite their own flaws.

When we embrace our imperfections, we awaken to another part of ourselves, that which had been neglected, unexplored and hidden behind lies, frustration, anger, miscommunications, and illusions of success and beauty.

Identity

I'm ok being me. In fact, I'm ecstatic about where my life is going, carrying every beauty mark and every blemish into my beautiful future. You, my sistas, must get to the place where you can genuinely express the same about your own perfected imperfections.

As you go on this journey be open to what is unfamiliar, some parts of you that you've never met may surface. So as you come face to face with the other parts of yourself, be cautious not to be too critical of what you discover. Remain open, examine, question, understand, grasp a hold of this unfolding, and grow to love it. Ultimately, you are the source to unlocking your best you. How you receive, reflect and respond, will shape your perception and determine your outcome.

A Reflection of My Father

Reflections of Your Identity

1. What does your name mean? If you are unsure, research it.

   _____
   _____
   _____
   _____
   _____
   _____
   _____
   _____
   _____

2. Do you find that in any way your name identifies who you are? If so, in what ways? If not, why?

   _____
   _____
   _____
   _____
   _____
   _____
   _____
   _____
   _____

Identity

3. If not, does the meaning in any way define someone you would like to be?

_____
_____
_____
_____
_____
_____
_____
_____
_____
_____
_____
_____

4. What *is* your perspective of yourself? Are you comfortable with who you are internally?

_____
_____
_____
_____
_____
_____
_____
_____
_____
_____
_____
_____

5. What things have shaped your existence the most?

6. What positive words do you remember the most?

Identity

7. What negative words do you hold on to the most?

8. Do you remember or rehearse the positive or negative words the most?

9. How will you change the tandem of negativity spoken to and over you?

_____
_____
_____
_____
_____
_____
_____
_____
_____
_____
_____
_____
_____

You are more than what you tell yourself. If it is a healthy positive, you are even more than that.

CHAPTER 4

Destined a Daughter

Born from chambers of stately abodes,
    through waters bearing life
Her arrival induces pounding hearts with fierce
    anticipation.
Her triumphant entry ignites joy that overflows,
And hearts are refashioned through eyes of grace.
Minds given the capacity to fathom a captured heart
    never imagined before.
Her existence redefines the love of her beholder.
Her cry drums the sound of fear from the transition,
From eternity into time, anticipation waits.
As she is received into arms of love, and calmness
    envelops her.
Stark cries, diminuendo to whimpers of comfort
    and amenity
Here is where she makes her mark
In this place, another journey begins…

I am because I was meant to be

IMPACT THE WORLD. It's what we were meant for. *Destined for greatness are* not just words we utter to inspire, but also to instill hope, that one may walk in greater purpose and affect the world in astounding and miraculous ways.

To see the manifestation of it is in part determined by your perseverance and grit to fulfill that purpose. No act is too small or grand, and no endeavor is too ambitious when we are moving toward our destiny, for each one is an upsurge in the path to fulfillment.

> *Daughters have not been able to basque in this because we as a whole have misunderstood the divine order of this structure and it's importance to a healthy people.*

As a daughter, we are meant to impact this world the way no one else can, and you, daughter, are in a very special place right now. The completion of our lives has been thought of with hope, and our future matters to more than to just you alone. Your contributions *in life* are essential to the continuance *of life*. A daughter is exactly who you were meant to be.

A daughter's presence can stir the hearts of the most stoic. It can soothe pains and calm souls, and it stills a brewing storm to render peace for all calm. Her very presence can fill the hopeless with hope. It encourages one to move mountains and fuel purpose.

Daughters ensure the health and posterity of mankind. Like a cradle, she soothes and safeguards, as she nourishes for longevity.

You carry nations in your wombs.

We give life after we bring forth life;
We speak life as a seed and
How we feed it determines its nourishment.
How we water it activates it.
How we treat it determines its resilience.
How we teach it sustains it.
How we love it helps it thrive.
We are ambassadors of life.
Life depends on your essence.

Daughters are to be productive, fill, grow, expand and spread the created goodness of who we are. There is a specific reason why you are here. Our existence is not to entertain an unseen, unknown, distant entity; we are not actors on a stage, in an alternate reality, nor are we just an afterthought of goodness.

You are, woman, female and as much as those are true, you also are a daughter. This truth never parts from our humanity. And this cycle of life must continue through you. To build successfully, you must be healthy.

As women, we've learned to wear many shoes and hold tightly to our titles. Our hats are embroidered with businesswoman, teacher, entrepreneur, clergy, entertainer, manager, saleswoman and the list go on. Though we walk in them with selfless pride, their impact has often been underrated. Through training, we've learned how to do our positions well and execute them excellently. By instruction, we're taught to be right for others. Through trials, challenges, and self helps, we learn to be better sisters, friends, wives, mothers. But a daughter. What shoes do you wear for that? Where do we obtain a crown of instruction for daughterhood? Where do we go to learn about the benefits of this title and relationship?

A daughter's womb is the conduit and vessel to all creation. Without you woman, doctors, lawyers, pastors, scientists, chefs, musicians, entrepreneurs, speakers, professors, white and blue collars, soldiers, generals, inventors, ***tribes, nations, kings,*** and other ***life bringers*** wouldn't exist.

You matter! Your life matters! We have too long denied ourselves the gift of being a daughter and relishing in the security of this status. Daughters have not been able to basque in this because we as a whole have misunderstood the divine order of this structure and it's importance to a healthy people.

Daughters are to be like graceful pillars cut for the structure of a palace. These pillars are to adorn. We are to enhance, bless and beautify wherever we are.

Being a daughter yields us to a place of submission, where others have authority over us. We may not like this thought, but it is true and beneficial to our emotional and mental health and growth. Without that opportunity, we miss crucial stages in our lives that go untapped, unnurtured, and unmatured.

It is in this special time of our lives we are taught how to give permission and to accept encouragement, validation, support, and protection. We begin to understand submission, not to man, but to discipline, to rest, guidance, and ultimately, to love.

She Needs Him, He Needs Her

Over the last century there has been a steady decline in the family structure; parents separated from one another, parents separated from their children, and children separated from each other, has become more of a *norm*.

With this decline, closer kinships have to be more intentional in building their connections. Individually, everyone is affected in some way if these bonds aren't formed.

Daughters have especially been uniquely affected by the miss or disconnect from the relationship with her father. The brokenness of their relationship hasn't allowed her to fully basque in the security of daughterhood. Part of the reasons may be because some parents may not have fully embraced their own positions and relationships in various stages of their lives, which can cause a struggle with the reality of the father-daughter relationship.

A Reflection of My Father

The severance from one she is a part of can make her liable to callousness or have her on a continual search for acceptance and love that won't get fulfilled until she faces the truth of her life, her feelings, her relationships, and herself. This insights the need a young girl has for her father's direction and wisdom. He shares the benefits she can experience with the fullness of the present father. Without it, she can witness the detriment that can exist when he is absent physically, mentally, and/or emotionally.

Something I know to be true, and I hope you will come to believe is that your contribution to this life *is* great, not just because I say it is, not only because I believe it is, but because I don't believe a creator would take the time to think us up without a divine purpose for us being here.

Greatness is found in the essence of your being. When others look at you, greatness *is* what they see. Your make-up is in the image of greatness, formed as a vessel of purpose, in the gift of daughterhood.

There is gravity in knowing who you are, your importance and your value. The awareness of worth strengthens your resolve in knowing that no one else can keep you from what you are to be.

Anything contrary to your truth, or that speaks negatively against it, attempts to convince you that you can't be free, you can't be whole, successful, loved, etc. The lies will frustrate your inner self, and if you let it, neutralize your potential. Why? Because our make-up is to be fruitful, productive and manifest, among other things.

When something clashes with whom you are naturally, it sends rifts, causing an internal struggle. You may not be able to pinpoint why everything within you is screaming one thing, while your mind keeps reverting to what you've heard, seen, or have been taught, but the struggle is for the lack of a better word, "real."

The inner you is trying to decide whether to fight for what you know with your whole being to be right for you or run away until you can figure in your mind how to manage what seems to be chaos.

Fight for your future or run to a comfortable, convenient place. Fight for your peace or revert to dissatisfaction.

Fight for your happiness or run to mediocrity.

Fight for destiny and purpose or run to the mere place of just existing.

Imagine your personal power given to someone else and they take that power and use it for wrong intent and purposes. The fruit of those ill intents are rotten and lacks to produce further. The results could be devastating to your future. And by no conscious or rational decisions of your own, your true destiny and divine purpose, your beatific, untold future, aborted.

You may accomplish some things and score small wins, but what you have been destined to fulfill and give to the earth has been lost by imperceptive or irrational judgments. Once more the enemy of our fruitfulness and destiny has exploited your gentleness and trust and gained another feat.

This is what can happen every time you decide to let your life happen without you. Each time you give over the authority to someone to make your life decisions for you. Ultimately the direction you take for your life is your decision. You are the only one who can determine if the road you take will be to fulfillment or to the adverse. I reiterate that whether it is by your own hands, or you allow the decisions for your life to be someone else's hands, you still choose which.

Shaped for Performance

It is defined in Merriam-Webster and The English by Oxford dictionaries and Dictionary.com that destiny is;

- The reason something exists
- Is the hidden power believed to control your future; fate
- Predetermined state, usually inevitable or irresistible course of events

Upon conception, our destiny is active. It is moving and is both present and future. It is now and to become.

In its present as in it is forming because we exist. All that we do is establishing our present position that sets us up for the next position.

Now–because no matter what, with every second destiny is being shaped.

Future–because it is going to happen despite anything.

Become–because we decide at every moment in every decision the road we take to our future.

In either case, who you are destined to be is shaped by every decision you make in your life. In you is the potential to be who have been created to be. Some things are beyond our control, and we learn to maneuver around or through them, but they are meant to happen, and we were meant to conquer them.

In other things, we have autonomy. We must realize that no matter how, when or by whom, decisions are being made about your life whether directly or indirectly. You are affected by them, even if they don't include your direct input. That hidden power to control your future is wrapped in your decisions. They determine what your tomorrow is and what you, in your tomorrow, will become. By them, your destiny becomes your reality.

I encourage you to choose today to be the one to make those decisions that move you forward in life. Your destiny awaits your instruction.

I am a daughter whose uniqueness, drive, love, gentleness, assertiveness, quirkiness, integrity, personality, intuitiveness, and innovativeness make a difference in this world. If I am absent from the equation, there is a void. No one will be able to bring to this life what I am to bring because there is only one me. If you haven't quite come to this, I hope that you soon will.

There is a purpose for all human existence. Every decision we make can move us forward in our purpose; as we move in purpose, it leads us closer to our predetermined place, one that is good and full of hope. No matter the twist and turns you may have made, when your heart is seeking, you shall find the answer to stay on the path to it, and every feat is a move toward fulfillment.

Many lessons we must learn along the way but through them, we get stronger, more resilient, more empathetic, wiser and the list goes on. Even when we're resistant to its teaching, we are still a part of its process. And destiny is all wrapped up in how we choose to respond to them.

In its predetermined state, we are, because we're unequivocally meant to be. That which is destined to be is and becomes. Not because we had a choice to be here, but because we were a part of the plan before we were imagined by procreators of life.

In reasoning for your existence there is purpose. You have been chosen to live this life. Created in beauty, at first sight of you, you were considered a good thing. There is no other like you. And though there may be a future that's not fully known, purpose can be found when we search for it and live life to its fullest.

For some, the reality of purpose may not even exist. It is not the goal to define your purpose for you. The aim is to transform your thoughts, or simply to remind you that there is a purpose and that you believe that there is a reason for you to be here. And the journey to discovering the what is just as exciting as coming to believe the why.

Unfortunately, not every child is received in loves arms. Not every daughter experienced the purity of love during their childhood.

The shocking reality is that the trust that is to bring these two closer may be broken at any moment. The number one offender is by his betrayal. Betrayal breaks the faith she has in his protection and his love. Because of it, rejection is a constant fear. Fear causes her to guard herself with an iron breastplate; nothing will penetrate it. It will also stunt her growth when it comes to having flourishing relationships, especially with other men.

Whether she is in one, and can't seem to fully trust, always thinking something is happening behind the scenes that will break her heart and end them, or she's moving in and out of those encounters for those same reasons, fear is the underline culprit to the unsteady and unfulfilling cycles. And though she yearns for someone to break

> *A father helps to establish her in her position, guards her soul and defends the sensitive, innermost parts of her that bear life.*

through and gain her trust, she makes it difficult for herself and for others.

The very opposite can be a result of her young experience also. How we respond to disappointing and tragic events depends on a person's personality and interpretation of them. They could regularly find themselves in comprising situations that endanger their physical, psychological and emotional self. And while this is not my story, every parent's experience or every child's reality, it happens all the time.

A Daughter, a woman, a lady, a girl, a female. All the words that define femininity and gender. Their meanings have been watered down, even cast aside at times. Our value to this world has been concealed beneath mounds of heaping coals, it's almost hard to find, and you'd have to get a skilled team to dig through the rubble and find those diamonds.

The truth of our purpose and essence of our nature has been lost in societal correctness. Our innocence has been mistreated, our beauty mishandled, our lives are open flames, and we've missed the confirmation in our position as a daughter. As children, we don't quite understand what it all means. We are as sponges, being programmed to hear what we are supposed to believe, and what happens to us is "just the way it is."

We haven't had the luxury of experiencing all being a daughter has to offer. But now is the time for that to change. We must be determined to take back what was stolen from us.

What we've heard since a child has been like a faint recorder in the back of our minds. The words, thoughts, and actions have helped shape not only what we believe about ourselves but about the world.

Our views can be reformed and renewed. We can turn what could have been used to render us powerless into the fuel to help us get our power back. It's not too late to experience the love you should have had as a little girl. By coming to fully love ourselves invites others to love us the same.

To Become Woman

An invaluable jewel being polished to brilliance

Our human make-up is remarkable and so wonderfully complex. A woman's existence is so great that her presence can create fear, love and a whole whirlwind of emotions. Our remarkability to adapt to any situation when necessary is demonstrated in our ability to almost master motherhood, career, marriage, and other relationships. It may take some time and practice, but we make it work, though it may look different for each of us.

The need for our father's care is inherent in us just as is the need to connect with other human beings. Our fathers have been given the blessed responsibility of molding us from the softness of our femininity into the strength of womanhood. Nourishment from a *healthy* relationship helps us to be strong, confident and righteous queens.

The status of a daughter entitles her to favorable treatment but also positions her to be groomed in this place as well. It gives her, woman, the permission to be submissive, in that she is safeguarded by love, and it allows her the susceptibility to one that has authority over her, not to control or rule, but to love and protect, the same way you should your own child.

It is a sensitive subject these days, submission and susceptibility, for it is looked upon as one who is weakened and timid. But I confer that it is only through the strength of knowing who you are, and what you carry, that a woman can be agreeably submitted, and to learn and accept love in its power.

This unacceptance began when we were little girls, and it carried through to adulthood. Either we don't allow ourselves, or we are denied the time to grow and develop into our identity as a woman. We are pushed or desire to step out into womanhood without understanding how to barely deal with our adolescence years or the softness of a lady.

By choice or by circumstance, when we haven't allowed ourselves to walk in the true distinctiveness of daughterhood - living in its light, we miss the nurturing our father is to give and that we rightfully deserve. We were intended to receive; strength, guidance, direction, confidence, security, and teaching.

What does it mean to live as a daughter? A father is to offer care and provision, leadership, support, and protection. He shows us through personal experience, what it is to be and feel secure, believing that no harm would come to us. He carries her out of danger into safety.

In our fathers' house is our time for guidance and insight that aids us in discovering our person as early as necessary. He aids in teaching us the value of our womanhood. One that embodies the beauty of life and allows us to utterly and completely revel in the unique and extraordinary identity in which you are to grow. Even the responsibility of a vow she makes is made void if her protector opposes, thereby keeping her future, reputation and her voice intact.

A daughters father helps to establish her in her position, guards her soul and defends the sensitive, innermost parts of her that bear life. With it, man's posterity is also preserved.

She is watched over as the jewel she is and kept chaste until her appointed time, when the responsibility is then relinquished to another, where he *should* find her, delighting in the comfort of her father's house.

When a woman or female at any age married, nations were bonded, and *she* represented the nations fruitfulness. If she is affected or threatened then so was life itself. If she is affected or threatened then so was life itself.

Without our father, whose example helps us to understand and more readily accept our position, we may struggle to triumphantly walk in our identity as a daughter. I write this with strong conviction, that a daughter needs to be able to remain and soak in the favor of her father's impartation.

If we refuse to even consider the nourishment the relationship gives, we can close ourselves to the benefits of healing and restoration in cases where we didn't have those experiences.

Stepping into our womanhood means more than getting through our giddy girly years. Let's be clear, this is not just determined by age. When I speak of womanhood, I am referencing a level of maturity that enables us to identify with our inner self, understand the joy and pains of developing love, and completely embracing yourself, your experiences, your life.

Having understood the importance of our purpose, it is clear that we are not to be put under a bushel, covered with a blanket or whisked aside. There is a light that can only shine through our eyes, through the brightness of our smiles, through the embrace of our arms, and through the life of our words. Coincidentally, our fathers should help secure us in these attributes for full expression, in the fullness of tenderness, knowledge, wisdom, and strength.

There's no doubt that hurt and pain will find its way, there's no denying that bricks will hit the road, and many lessons are to be learned for our growth. But it is an atrocity when we must learn these life lessons without his guidance we were intended to have. Without it, we become malnourished in areas of our lives where we should be thriving.

Jewels undergo an intense purification process. Just like these gems, you may experience bruising, tossing, tugging, scuffing and scathing, only to be prepared and presented as that rare jewel shining in brilliance and made stronger and stronger. These experiences can render one exhausted, and undaunting, not wanting to stand with the tenacity or courage in the battles ahead, but remember amid it all, a woman will continue to grow and build. A wise one builds with both hands, at her level, in every stage, and can see fruitfulness, nurturing in gentleness, courage and tenacity.

The affection I have for my father is as real as me rising each morning. He helped me to appreciate the beautiful responsibility of loving myself that I may also love others. To allow myself to be all that I am, anywhere, all the time, and not to shrink in the presence of greatness because I too am great.

As I look at myself through the mirror, I see me. I see what others see when they look at me. I see beauty and grace, love and kindness, strength and power. I see him that has given me life, and the One that has breathed life.

A Daughter After His Heart

Imagine if you can, the heartbeat of love that calms every storm, even if it's just our perspective of one. To

A Reflection of My Father

our rescue, comes our knight in shining armor. Clothed in luminous garments and appearing in the light of our father. As he appears, fear dissipates and safety envelopes us, each and every time.

As infants, we learn images of genuine intelligence and begin to experience senses of basic trust and mistrust. Every time he comes to our rescue or fails to, trust is being confirmed or exploited.

When our fathers appear, we expect him over and over again. When he fails us, we are left with an emptiness unexplained. In both cases, we are continuously searching for that love, that was either given or that we feel missing.

When the opportunity is stripped from us, we miss the advantages of being able to basque in the security of daughterhood. If those moments are missed, our hearts can become fragmented, and only pieces of us shine forth in moments when more of us should.

I read a book once by Jack Frost called "Experiencing the Fathers Embrace." He shared how a person's relationship can be influenced by the lack of or the presence of a natural father. That book compelled me to ponder more about this the year I read it.

It caused me to think even deeper about my own relationship with my father. And then other experiences (mine own and others.) Some who didn't have a great relationship with their fathers. Others who never knew them and only live with the pseudo idea of what a father is or should be.

Maybe you've considered this, or maybe not much at all, but what does having a *man* in your life look like when you haven't had much of an example, even less no personal examples?

We can fail to conceive the concept of a father's love, a fathers' embrace, protection, or guidance. We don't know what healthy fraternal support, encouragement or validation looks like.

It is then we try to mirror the fairytales of storybooks and television shows. We try to envision, then create lives that we've seen exampled, only to find our own lives turned upside down. Why? Because the truth is, your father, or the man, or beau hasn't had the same experiences, haven't lived the same lives, or lived with the same type of family members and friends shown in the movies. His experiences are far different from what you dream they are. His experiences may have kept him from being able to fully embrace their own life.

In recent generations, I've noticed the respect we once had for authority, leadership and love has transformed into a game of power, control, and lust. Nowadays, girls don't seem to have the reverence for their fathers as they once did for many, many reasons today.

Yet, some subsequently look for men that essentially will fill the shoes of the man they didn't respect (think about that for a moment.) She still desires that love whether she speaks it or not.

A Reflection of My Father

So the searching continues for a man like her daddy, or for a man she may have thought her daddy was, and all she feels she deserve, trying to fill the voids with those illusionary ideas of the perfect one.

The breakdown in daughterhood means there's brokenness in identity, and individualism strives to act on its own with little guidance and structure. We lose who we are supposed to become, trying to find a place to fit in society.

As we look at what's plaguing our society, we will notice the absent, less important position the father has played in the family structure. The bottom line is, if the healthy examples of fatherhood are restored, we are on our way to family restoration. Complete family health and the restoration of the father-daughter dynamic.

This restoration will foster a smooth transition into other relationships. But if the transition is difficult, other areas could be challenging.

If we seek after what is right and good in this bond, we will find our identity in a safe place, under the protection of our fathers, and society will find a way for us to be a part of it. It has no choice but to fit us in so to speak.

Reflections on Destined a Daughter

1. Why do you think you exist?

   _____
   _____
   _____
   _____
   _____
   _____
   _____
   _____
   _____
   _____

2. Do you believe the love or lack of it influenced these views? If so, in what ways?

   _____
   _____
   _____
   _____
   _____
   _____
   _____
   _____
   _____

A Reflection of My Father

3. Who and what has shaped your life?

___

4. Do you believe that how you see yourself has affected your relationships with others?

___

5. What are your self-views?

6. What type of people are you most drawn to?

A Reflection of My Father

7. What kind of men are you drawn to?

8. Does this (#7) in any way reflect your relationship or lack of with your father?

9. What does destiny mean to you?

___

10. Do you know what you are destined for?

___

You can accomplish it.

CHAPTER 5

A Reflection of His Presence

Your presence is like the sun,
it brightens the cloudy days.
Illuminate the place hidden in the night,
the darkness cannot run from your light
The energy you radiate empowers my being.
I am warm, energized and not afraid to shine.
By your light, mine own is reflected.

One of the most important things for a woman, aside from love, is to feel safe and secure. When she does there is a comfort in knowing that she is sheltered from harm. It allows her to relax in the moments and enjoy her present. Safety is a luxury that many women haven't experienced.

Our fathers should be our first protector in our natural lives. His presence should bolster the safety every girl should feel. He is the one who guides us into understanding and his presence should offer peace, reassuring her that she's taken care of, provided for, any danger will be kept at bay, and she has a shield to quench the fiery darts with love.

Her father is her defense. He will stand when she is unable to or doesn't know to. She doesn't have to fight because he will fight on her behalf. In that, she is free and safe to be who she is in that moment and moments forward, unto a continual discovery of who she is becoming.

He brightens her gloomy days, shines the light on the dark places, energizes her atmosphere, charging her to stand in the light that is reflected by his own.

You were there, and you are still

As the sun rose, so did my expectation of what the day would bring. When I was younger that day meant I would spend time with daddy and that was good for me.

I always wanted to be in my father's presence (except when I was out having other fun) no I wasn't thinking about it day and night so don't think this weird obsession with my father. However, I knew that when I went home, I would be around daddy. I always expected him to be there, but I always wanted him near as possible. He didn't have to say anything; I could just sit around him all day. He was warm and loving, and I couldn't resist smiling when he smiled.

We can all too often take a father's presence for granted. When my father went somewhere I wanted to go. When he went to work I wished he was home and wondered what took him so long getting back.

When I think of heaven, I see the clouds lighter than cotton. I can let my pretty feet sink in and it's the softest thing they've ever felt.

I see streets of gold. With every step, there is sparkle dust that dances into the air. Seas of glass reveal the colors of the rainbow in florals, butterflies, and greenery.

I'm beautiful, I glow, my face highlighted, shimmering from my substance. My dress flows beautifully amid the breeze. Joy flows from me and my heart is content. I see his smile. I hear his laughter. I feel happy.

Heaven is what I felt when I was with my daddy. There was an inner joy that I cannot explain, and being a woman of few words, I wouldn't dare try.

For a long time, and even as in writing this, I'm discovering it still, I wasn't allowing myself to experience heaven anymore.

> *Holding on to the pain won't let our idea of heaven on earth in. Bring yourself to experience heaven*

The memories are still there, and I can see it all, but I don't feel it. With every pleasant thought every smile that extends my face, my heart hurts. Missing this love.

I can only make the best of his absence. Heaven can be serene and glorious, but holding on to the pain of loss won't let heaven in. So I bring myself to experience heaven once again. The joy and appreciation of having my father for the time is one of my greatest gifts.

A Reflection of My Father

A daughter's cry of a heart is wanting her father to show his love, to give his support and if he doesn't know how to give her that, she wants him to at least be there.

His presence can be felt even when he's far away, just as a father can still be there and not be present or active in your life.

My father has always been there, no matter the distance I always knew I had access to him. I have a reverential fear that I have known since I can remember. Respect and adoration are second nature and there is no questioning who my biggest crush was.

You may have been on either one side or the other and some of you may have experienced both. Yes, having a presence is about being there mentally, emotionally and/or whenever possible physically.

My father didn't always have to be with me physically; his presence was felt even in his physical absence. The gravity of a father's active presence is more powerful and effectual than one can imagine. Seen or unseen, his presence is always noticed. No matter the proximity, his presence, should be felt. It should have a physical, emotional & social impact that extends far beyond his physical location.

For those who find this difficult to comprehend, it means that even if your father isn't there in location, the spirit of him should be felt and experienced, if he has made an impact on your life. The same honor, respect, and reverence that has been developed should remain as if he was there physically.

As I mentioned before, if a person didn't have the experience of their father's presence, they may subconsciously try to create a sense of it. This is not to place a blame on anyone. We should keep in mind that our parents, including our fathers, may be experiencing the same type of issues and have themselves struggled to understand how crucially important it is to be a part of a child's life. Individuals and circumstances are different, and the dynamics are not always known so we never know how a person is affected by their upbringing and experiences. This may be the very reason why these things were missing from our life, they didn't get it and failed to learn how to give it. Yes, men experience this too, which is the main reason we should mention it here. They can express their lack of love and absence in many of the same ways, but that's a different book.

When a person hasn't received something themselves they find it to be a great challenge to give it to others. It takes healing, forgiveness and their own process of getting pass that void in their own lives.

In his presence, you feel you can be and do anything. In his absence, you've missed the impartation of love, selflessness, assurance, and security. In dissonance, you have the same type of struggles as with an absent father. A physical presence doesn't mean there is guidance and support. A dad can be there and hardly ever engage with his child. This could result in her feeling even less wanted or loved.

A Reflection of My Father

There is no question of whether a father's natural presence matters in the lives of his children. For both son and daughter, the impacts are both felt and seen.

For those who were fortunate to have your father around, whether biological or not, glean all you can.

For those experiencing deep and seemingly unexplainable emotions because of your father's absence, what you're missing will be restored to you.

You who have had that love replaced, one who that stepped in and didn't miss a beat, inherently depositing the love that is intended and necessary for you, give thanks.

A Reflection Of His Presence

Reflections of His Presence

Take some time to think about how your relationship or its absence with your father changed your life.

1. Was your father present, and was he active?

   _____
   _____
   _____
   _____
   _____
   _____
   _____
   _____
   _____

2. How did this affect you?

   _____
   _____
   _____
   _____
   _____
   _____
   _____
   _____
   _____
   _____

A Reflection of My Father

3. Do you think it's affected your relationship with those around you?

   _____
   _____
   _____
   _____
   _____
   _____
   _____
   _____
   _____
   _____
   _____

4. Has it impacted your relationship with your spouse or your mate?

   _____
   _____
   _____
   _____
   _____
   _____
   _____
   _____
   _____
   _____
   _____

5. Did you feel loved? Why or why not?

6. Are there some things you wish you would have gleaned more from you dad? What were they?

7. What are some thoughts about your relationship with your father as you read this chapter?

_____
_____
_____
_____
_____
_____
_____
_____
_____
_____

8. What are some other thoughts you are having in this moment?

_____
_____
_____
_____
_____
_____
_____
_____
_____
_____

Your gift still awaits.

CHAPTER 6

A Reflection of His Love

Love created me, and I exist.
Love shapes me, and I become.
Love nourishes my soul, and I learn.
Love captures my heart, and I grow.
Love gives wings and I soar.
Love loves me, and I love.

One of the greatest loves that have impacted my life is that of my parents. Now being a parent, I understand what it is to hold your newborn child in your arms for the first time. What it means to love another human being more than you ever thought you could, to be willing to give your everything, so they could have it all.

My parents nurtured and have embraced my life since conception. I was a healthy baby and healthy child and since I've grown, my decisions have been in mine own hands. I'd like to believe I've learned, grown and now make the best decisions to live a healthy adult life, in both my physical and spiritual wellbeing, in relationships, and in love.

The endearment a father expresses to his daughter that she is wanted for who she is, is priceless. I could find hundreds of quotes about how he feels about her, but to experience it or to be the object of that endearment, fills life with treasure that can never be totally forgotten.

I've heard, read, and have said myself that a father is a girls first true love, and indeed he should be. However, that reality can quickly fade or cease to exist for some of us.

Whether he was gone from the beginning or leaves, it is a sad reality that continues, and because of it, many girls and women, young and old miss out on the blessing of relishing in her father's love.

I remember my father's exuberance when he saw us. He gave a soothing smile, and it was almost as if he was just smiling at me (because again in my mind, I was his favorite). I could almost hear his love through his smile. He would extend his arms, welcoming my presence. As I responded to his beckon, I felt the comfort of being wanted, by him whom I absolutely adored. His embrace made me feel safe and melted my heart. He then landed this weeeeeet kiss on my cheek. I most certainly felt his love long after the experience. The wet cheek was a reminder!

That was my dad. I knew that he loved me (yes my sisters too), and I was his favorite girl. These experiences repeated throughout my life. Even as I got older, the love he expressed and the way he expressed it was no less than when I was younger, and my adoration for him only increased.

If this sounds like a piece of a love story, my goal is accomplished, because it is. One of a girl, who loved her daddy more than she could ever express. But, the most amazing part is that he loved me first!

Love is such a **strong** word. While identity and validation are pillars, love *is* the foundation. Love allows identity and validation to achieve their goals while their purposes are being accomplished. Without love, identity is (as my mom used to say) a hard paymaster and being validated is an attempted duty without its purpose being accomplished.

Without love, searching for identity will resemble a sound as heavy as the trombone, sinking beneath the crevices in uncertainty. Validation will be as a cymbal that crescendos to reverberated clanging blares. They each are noises not soon quieted.

It's loves genuineness and compassion from a pure place that allows love to flow. The hearts motivation cannot be concealed, and the intent of validity and identity can be easily translated. It needs to be the foundation for everything we have and discuss.

The foundation of love can be challenged, but true love can't be torn down or broken if we hold fast to it. Love holds an extraordinary weight, extends to the highest height, and delves the deepest depths. On love is where a sure foundation is built.

And the Greatest of These

I have found that when people are discussing *love*, they often define the outward expressions rather than love itself. There are many **concepts** of love, and the meaning translates differently depending on the carrier or the receiver.

Dictionary.com and The Free Dictionary by Farlex state it like this:

- *A strong affection for another arising out of kinship or personal ties*
- *maternal love for a child*
- *warm <u>attachment</u>, enthusiasm, or devotion*
- *unselfish loyal and benevolent concern for the good of another: such as*
  - *the fatherly concern of God for humankind*
  - *brotherly concern for others*
  - *a person's adoration of God*

You can clearly see by the definitions, there are varying levels, attributes, occasions and feelings of love. An *unselfish loyal and benevolent concern* is the closest to help determine its value and define its true meaning. Because we "feel" a certain way, doesn't prove that love is present. If we love, we do feel most of the time, but feelings change as do emotions, and the heart is deceitful, who can know it? The heart can be blinded by our perceptions of love and the emotions we feel only compounds those feelings of it. Love is more than just a feeling or emotion.

Some even equate love to be an action or calls it an action word. Though love compels you to act, *love* far exceeds action. The facts are, we can act without love, so action doesn't authenticate love.

On the other hand, what's even more truer is that it's hard to love without acting. Those actions are outward demonstrations of the innermost conviction, but if not careful, one can devalue the meaning of love to simple actions or something you feel. Even though love is the motivation behind the act, these things are only by-products of love.

At the same time, there seems to be a lack of love being expressed for people to identify with the desires of its' reality. It is easy for one to assume that if you love, you give. But this doesn't by any means complete the full meaning of the text, because there can be many reasons for giving. If you look at its deeper meaning, we will see that giving is just the by-product of what love is. We don't love because we give, but we do give because we love. Get it?

Attempting to define *love* by explaining its characteristics or attributes doesn't give it the full justice it deserves. My understanding and revelation of love are homologous to most. When I consider its function, I meditatively conclude that love is a power. It is an unmovable force that covers, protects, sharpens, develops, supports, cares for, values, appreciates, validates, encourages, endures, brings joy, challenges, comforts and so, so, so much more. Whether I feel it or not, it exists, and it is real.

> *Love is a power, an unmovable force that covers, protects, sharpens, develops, supports, cares for, values, appreciates, validates, encourages... and so much more*

Love—a power and an unmovable force, remember that. When we have it, we are unstoppable. But when one is without it, the question of it ripples through their life, sending endless waves of distrust and suspicion.

One of the most famous sayings that I'm aware of is found in the most popular book of all time, the Bible.

Love suffers long and is kind; love does not envy; love does not parade itself, is not puffed up; does not behave rudely, does not seek its own, is not provoked, thinks no evil; does not rejoice in iniquity, but rejoices in the truth; bears all things, believes all things, hopes all things, endures all things.

Love never fails.

Before I ever knew where they were from, I had thought they were some of the most beautiful words I'd ever heard. I was in my teens then and it still rings true. No wonder why they're so popularly quoted at one of the most celebrated life events one could experience. The coming together in powerful covenant.

It gives us both loves traits and shares love's intrinsic nature. It also tells us what love is *not*. As I meditate upon these words, I see a love that never gives up, and no matter the trials, it endures, and it always wins. It may not always feel or look good when faced with it, and sometimes it may downright stink, but it still wins.

By omission, it says that if you are showing these, you are *not* displaying love. Your influence or motivation for action is derived from a different power than that of love.

Those words are preceded by these;

And though I bestow all my goods to feed the poor, and though I give my body to be burned, but have not love, it profits me nothing.

That tells me no matter what anyone or I do if I don't have love it doesn't account for anything. See, more than an action.

I can't help but think that my stance here may lead one to interpret that I am encouraging you to deal with anything if there is love. Let me clarify. If what you experience does not currently display or is developing into the definition of what is written, you must question the authenticity of the relationship, with ANYONE!

The word is used so loosely, in passivity and in shallowness. When some people are asked what love means to them, many respond with answers of ambiguity. They cannot give a direct answer because they do not fully know and understand what love is.

Most times, people respond with what love isn't, and of course, these responses are based on personal relationship experiences and are more directed towards the expressions or its content instead of its essence.

This is not inappropriate or inaccurate, in fact we often define things by our experiences. It is just as asking someone what they want in life, they usually respond by telling you what they don't want.

Seldom do we take the time to think about the experiences we want to have. But we can tell you what we don't want? This is what we've experienced over our lifetime. A mound of don't wants. But how many can tell you what they *do* want. The answers come with experiencing what you should have, being a witness to it, or actively thinking about it, just as you do with the things you refuse to have.

Love is an extension of self. Its expressions are influenced by genuineness, and its objective is to nurture, develop and liberate.

Patience allows me to grow beyond my immaturity and fault.

Kindness deters wrath that can stir up for many reasons.

It does not envy because love wants me to do my best and have the best and is not threatened by it.

Does not boast because loves motivation is pure.

Is not proud because it doesn't need to seem more than it is.

Does not dishonor, so it doesn't make you feel bad or unworthy because of it.

Is not self-seeking do it doesn't demand personal recognition or demand return for giving it

Not easily angered so it isn't exasperated by your shortcomings.

Keep no account of wrongs, so it forgives to no end and continues to love despite wrongdoings.

Does not delight in evil so love is not satisfied or comfortable with injustices

Rejoices in truth so it is happy with honesty and truth and accepts it fully.

Always protect, so it watches over your wellbeing, wards off danger and covers you.

Always trust, so it has faith to believe that your best will manifest in and through you.

Always hope, so it looks forward to the light that will shine no matter what you experience, and it encourages you in that.

Always preserve, so it is willing to endure or undergo whatever it needs to on your behalf.

The bottom line is, you don't love because you display these attributes, but because you love are all these displayed. Very different.

In its' essence love is purely and wholeheartedly giving of yourself to another. Its expressions embody patience, kindness, endurance, does not envy, bears, hopes, believe, isn't prideful or doesn't rejoice in iniquity.

I believe with all my being that I am loved. I recognize it from my childhood. A father's love, regardless of what our future holds, keeps us strong, keeps us hopeful, it keeps us wanting to experience more.

Still looking for His Heart

While we as women may desire to have that knight-in-shining-armor romance, or hopeless romantic storybook ending, it is not always our reality.

Our experiences have told us that love is painful, and it is ecstatic, foolish and realistic, the greatest and the worst. The truth is that love is none of these things. Love loves you through these moments. We may encounter these things during our quest for it, but what we experience are only results of their true sources-human desire, hurt, pain, unmet expectations, rejection, etc., not love.

Let me explain; if my desire to have love in my life is strong, I can pursue love because of the love I received from my father. In my pursuit to find it, I can encounter heartbreak if I can't obtain it in the same or greater capacity. The heartbreak occurs not because that's what love does, but because of my human desire to have it, unmet expectations of no longer receiving it and the impatience of waiting for love to find me.

A Reflection Of His Love

Love, by far, is the most important ingredient to add to one's life. It is love that compels us to give of ourselves and pour out of ourselves, extending to the end of self, for someone else.

However, the reality quickly fades or has never existed for some of us. It is a sad reality that continues, and because of it, many girls and women, young and old miss out on the essential molding and makings of their true selves.

If I were to sum this up in reference to what we are discussing, love is simply about others–being selfless. Something even a father must learn how to be. Then with every fiber of his being, pour that selfless love on us.

I remember one of my sisters speaking at my father's homegoing, as she spoke, *"Everything he did, he did in love. Even when he disciplined, he disciplined in love."* I felt the words ring through my soul, and I latched onto them so much that I often speak them as if I authored them–*even when he disciplined, he did it in love*–because they spoke volumes about my father.

I could always feel love from him, even through the telephone. He could be hundreds of miles away, and it was like he was living in the same house. When he spoke, I listened, and I dared not go against his word. I not only knew him, but he lived in my heart, my mind, and as far as I was concerned, he could be living in my house with me.

His compassion for us was overwhelming. Make no mistake though, his love was not blinding. My dad's love is what gave him the authority to apply the necessary discipline and encourage his children to be better and to become more than what they saw with the naked eye.

Lack of **love** breeds destruction. People will search for it all their lives if they need to, not knowing what it looks or feels like. It is like a stranger; so when approached by love, we run from it and cleave to what love isn't.

A daughter not receiving it early on deprives her of the competences to understand love and its capacity-she may struggle in relationships, and even in her very own existence.

Loves absence for extended periods can undoubtedly produce feelings of insecurity, rejection, mistrust, neglect, being unloved and unlovable. Our inability to reliably identify these common issues can cause us to negligently forge unhealthy connections. Coasting through these relationships, we unveil how the stability of an authentic connection is undermined.

We are left with a sense of self – preservation that cautions us not to proceed even in absence of harm, false securities, and the tendency to overcompensate in the illusion of confidence–engulfing ourselves in the lives of our loved ones, our careers, hobbies and other things, to cover up the loneliness and untrustworthiness we hold.

When a person feels what they equate to love is distant or absent, what becomes attached is hate or some form of it–fear, insecurity, rejection, etc. Their presence become the primary existence in their reality and drifts into their relationships.

You struggle to understand what love is supposed to be or feel like is real. We then can easily begin to try and mimic what we have seen as love, creating our own realities, only to be disappointed time and time again.

We can become depressed, experience feelings of oppression, loneliness, and exclusion, because no one can quite give you what you've been waiting and longing to experience.

You may certainly have a heart and compassion for others, and though you desire to be loved, your experience with love has kept you in a distant place. You socialize, you smile, laugh, converse, advise, empathize all the while unintentionally distancing yourself to avoid any displeasure that is familiar, at the same time pushing away any pleasure of real relationships.

There is a disconnect. And it will have you feeling abandoned and unable to trust others with your heart. You'll unquestionably offer your helping hand where there is need because of a natural compassion for human life.

You'll give them your head, offering the best advice and direction that help move them to a better position in their own lives. But your heart is only for you, partially lending it only to very few.

To some you seem fulfilled (and you may be in most areas.) to others; wise, fake, or an arrogant know it all. They, not recognizing your vulnerabilities, possibly because of their own issues with love.

As we move to change, we will be exposed. As it happens, true love can move in. There is thankfulness to knowing that our ability to *be* loved and *feel* love, is not limited to our experiences *of* love. And what's even more rich and fulfilling is that a person's expressions of love is not the ultimate expression of love.

Reflection on Reflections of His Love

1. What does love mean to you?

   _____
   _____
   _____
   _____
   _____
   _____
   _____
   _____
   _____
   _____

2. Was your idea of love different than what is shared in this chapter?

   _____
   _____
   _____
   _____
   _____
   _____
   _____
   _____
   _____
   _____

3. What were your examples of love?

4. When do you feel the most loved?

5. Who makes you feel loved most? Why?

6. Do you feel that you received the love that you needed from your father?

A Reflection of My Father

7. Do you believe that the love or lack of love you received has caused negative or positive self-views? If so, in what ways?

   _____
   _____
   _____
   _____
   _____
   _____
   _____
   _____
   _____
   _____
   _____

8. How will your current understanding about love change your views, behaviors and treatment of it?

   _____
   _____
   _____
   _____
   _____
   _____
   _____
   _____
   _____
   _____
   _____

Remember that Love Never Fails.

CHAPTER 7

A Reflection from His Validation

Before we get into it, I want to make a point that I believe is necessary because as we move forward in this chapter we should understand that love, as we mentioned in the previous chapter, is the foundation for all we discuss.

We can easily misinterpret arrogance for confidence. But validation without love is a recipe that breeds false confidence in need of a reality check, specifically for

> *Your words have power, to the life of one or to the death of another. Choose to speak life. Build. Edify. Restore. Give love. Impart validity.*

the receiver. It is because validation builds, exalts, and given often enough, can puff up, but love grounds. Love shows you how to humbly accept approval without it fueling conceit.

Profuse validation given without love's foundation is building on dangerous ground. It creates a sense of stability only in what you have been reassured in. At some point, love must come in and cushion the checkpoints.

At the same time validation is hard to give without love or adoration existing in some dimension. Validation, otherwise, would be just empty words from the giver. But the one that hears them coming from either place will grasp every word spoken.

Approved for this world

Since love is the foundation on which these attributes derive, then validation is certainly within the walls. In fact, it is a cornerstone that helps offer stability and is upheld by its sure foundation, love. Validation is an act of that foundation, or think of it like this, validation is an attitude of love that is instilled.

Validation given throughout our lives is most prominent in two instances, childhood and our teen years. Teen years are the times when what was given to you in childhood is affirmed and reaffirmed repeatedly.

As children, we remember what was said to us and we experience the spirit in which it is said. We can feel the emotions of love, anger, sadness, jealousy and every emotion behind the words through tones, and language, even if we can't articulate them.

A Reflection From His Validation

Those words and the spirit in which they were spoken begin to shape us. If it is constant, we begin to rehearse and believe these words, outside of make-belief.

If you remember the story, I shared in chapter 3 about how my sister's friend shared such mean words about how pretty I was up to my smile. While her words were downright critical, she said them with a smile on her face, and in a mild tone, and I felt every word she said.

Even though she was still a young teenager, you have to realize that the words you speak carry life or death. Her words could have been the death of my confidence, my perspective of my own beauty and the view of one of my most valuable aesthetic assets. Yet, while life was consistently breathed into me, I had to constantly combat death through those words for my confidence. Could you imagine if these words would have been spoken by one who has had the responsibility for my life since birth?

Even now, though I am free of their effect, I still remember those words. They are reminders that I will find the beauty in all my sisters, my brothers, and in every creature upon this earth. Out of them birthed the awareness to not hurt another living being by what I speak. Remember your words have power, to the life of one or to the death of another. Choose to speak life. Build. Edify. Restore. Give love. Impart validity.

Validation is powerful. It is essential to building confidence to do, be and become.

A Reflection of My Father

Do–everything that you aim to. Even in the face of fear, challenges, and resistance.

Be–Being who you are in the moments. Taking each moment at a time and finding solace and joy in them.

Become–Aspire for more. Be not afraid to be yourself and stretch beyond your right now. Understanding, the more you desire to experience is within you, and preparing, always preparing, to experience that expansion. It only ceases when you decide to stop searching and just exist in your moment.

My father was intentional with making sure I believed in myself and letting me know that he believed in me as well. I think his ultimate goal in that, was to help me understand that I don't need to depend on anyone, I have everything in me to accomplish what I want to obtain in life. When I was younger, I remember him telling me "you can be anything you want to be", "You can do anything you want to do.

His statements ring in my head more often than I can tell you. When I need to be reminded, it is his voice I hear telling me *you can*. And do you know what? I believed him! I absolutely, undoubtedly believed him! If I need to hear it audibly, my husband never fails. He encouragingly echoes my dad, *you can*.

I thought that there was nothing I could not do if I wanted to. Yes, there may be things that seemed a little challenging, but I still believed I could do them because my dad said I could, and no one could tell me otherwise.

A Reflection From His Validation

Not only would my father speak this, but he trusted that what he was teaching me was real, to me. I remember being a young girl at the beginning of my elementary school years. We were sitting at our kitchen table where one of my older sisters had algebra homework. She couldn't figure it out. After going through the assignment with her, my dad sat to show me how to figure it and I got it immediately! I was so excited, and I thought because I caught on so easily that it was just easy to do, and I didn't understand why it was so difficult for them.

I was a cheerful and energetic little girl. When I was testing for school, I couldn't keep still. As the teachers were trying to instruct me to settle down, stop moving and concentrate, my father gestured them to not disturb *me*. When my test scores were received they all were shocked that I was in the high 90th percentile (if I remember correctly)!

My father helped me to believe that I was extremely smart. I knew beyond a shadow of a doubt that I could accomplish anything that I put my mind to. Though I've always been a pretty quiet, non-boastful person, my heart still pumps confidence in my ability to succeed when the effort is put forth.

I share this to say that because of what my father declared over my life in my hearing has stayed with me, and I am persuaded to that declaration. It's something I'll hold on to for the rest of my life.

If you're validated early in your childhood, your confidence in those areas of authentication is resolute. Validation is very important to fulfillment in your lives. If you don't have it, you can accomplish so much and still feel like you're missing something.

Validation says, "I" matter. When a father validates his daughter, it builds her confidence with every declaration. It affirms her existence as a girl, a lady, and a woman. It is an edict that she will hold on to, because it plays in her head, and her heart believes its truths.

Validity positions us to pursue our passions in the spirit of wholeness. While many things can fuel the drive to accomplishment, his validation almost assures it.

To our visions of success, a father's validation can instill a healthy idea of accomplishment, and keep the fire burning, rather than her having to get refueled by seeking acceptance from outside sources.

Let's explore love without validation. If you've had love in the home and haven't been assured in that, there can still be a lingering sense of questioning of self in some areas. We call it, insecurity.

We need to be assured who we are in that love. Even when you recognize what love is, and you know you're loved, even engulfed in it, you will be confident in some areas, but still struggle in other areas to be enough, if you're not validated. And if there is insecurity because of a lack of validation, we can even struggle to receive or accept that love being given, because we need to hear it. And it doesn't matter who you are.

Love should be at the heart of things. It is the strong foundation, and everything else needs to be built on that love. The other attributes help us to be sure and confident in who we are and who you've been created to be.

With love missing, you're likely to still seek that something that validates you. Because it is in love, where validation stands. But even when you're loved, you can still find yourself in unhealthy relationships because you're trying to find validation in them, attempting to make up in areas where she hadn't been validated, imposing unjust expectations and demands on others to satisfy her personal deficiencies.

In this, the importance of validation is to build trust and confidence and confirm and reaffirm her beauty, intelligence and the greatness she already possesses. It upholds and that personal power remains.

Validate is a word that spews confidence and worthiness. It empowers her; her decisions are sound in those areas; she is confident in her appearance, no matter how ragged her sweats or wild her hair. Even in areas where she'll be challenged, she feels at minimum, capable.

When presented to her, it helps keep her content with her reality, whatever it may be. She doesn't become desperate to fill her atmosphere with false securities that appear to satisfy the longing for attention, acceptance, and admiration.

She will, very rarely, find herself trying to prove to herself, and others, that she is worthy. She will rarely lack the confidence to stand, even if alone, in her moments.

These are the very things that a father fills her with through affirmation. When her father imparts, it strengthens the believability and says, ***you don't have to look outside of what you've been given to feel worthy, validity is within you***!

It keeps us from seeking it from other sources at the varied stages and in varying capacities in our lives, whether it's in a personal relationships with friends, workplace, spouse, in crowds, or in titles and positions, all which only gives us temporary satisfaction, if any at all.

For example, you may feel completely confident to do your job because you are knowledgeable and have the to-do spirit to do it well. Or at socializing because you have trained yourself how to talk to people, but the struggle to maintain close relationships with those of the same sex, opposite sex or both, is still there. Minimal or the absence of validation could produce an underlining belief that you will fall short and others will not accept who you are.

You need to hear that you are. When you don't; you wonder, you question, you doubt, you emotionally attach to the idea that there is something you must do to gain acceptance or approval. You continue in what you've become used to, drowning yourself in work, or being the life of the party, demanding the attention you need without developing relationships that go beyond praising you for whom you seem to be.

The intent here is not to say that we can't build relationships, only that when you try, something gets in the way of allowing you to draw closer.

There can be a fear of others seeing you for who you are, your true joys, feelings, your fears. It keeps you close enough to laugh, give sound advice, share surface information and have unessential conversations, but keeps you distant enough to "get out" when you decide the pressure to *get closer* is too much.

Yes, all of this can occur from the lack of feeling worthy, stemming from not being validated. Validity helps us confirm our position in our purpose and keeps us moving forward to destiny.

Even, if at any point, you step out of or are drowned out of alignment, eventually identity, validation and love's foundation, will snap you back. You will say, *wait a minute, this is not who I am,* and you will begin to refuse to accept anything that does not edify you.

It positions us to pursue our passion and purpose. Many triggers that can fuel the tenacity to become, but sometimes those triggers can contaminate. You can begin to create a toxic atmosphere, for others and yourself.

Validation without love may also yield a higher chance of shortage of a woman's empathy to another person's feelings and situations. Arrogance convinces her to believe she's better, always criticizing, thinking she has the "answer" and she develops an imaginary sense of importance, not to herself but to others.

With every effort, every challenge, we release energy. Toxins and toxicity levels can scale dangerously high. Those that enter the atmosphere will be affected by it, but no one more than you.

My motto to combat is ***Burn clean***. Put the negativity through the fire to be burned. Process your thoughts, the words, the feelings, all that you rehearse, before you release the frustrations in public and impersonal spaces.

Change your inner voice to transform your heart. Make decisions filtered through processed, healthy thoughts and whatever the motivation when you release, educe healthy extraction.

A father's voice helps a daughter to believe the voice she hears. The voice that has repeatedly said, "you're beautiful, you're worth it, you can do anything." When she faces challenges or obstacles are in her way, the echo becomes her voice. She hears the words "even as her own voice, and she then believes. She trusts that "yes, she can."

Rejecting Rejection

My experiences in life made me very independent, almost to a fault. I was very comfortable being

A Reflection From His Validation

by myself, and that can make one seem a little cold and disconnected.

While internally I was more connected than anyone I knew and had so much compassion and empathy for others. Externally, my posture exhibited pretentiousness. No one knew how introverted I was and still am, but that's a whole *nother* topic, for another day.

What's interpreted by others is what opens the door for them to draw near or turn away. After it was shared with me how others saw me, I could choose to believe that motives were impure and ingenuine for wanting to be close to me, and continue to let them believe I was a boujee to keep them away, or I could carefully approach it a more positive light.

Rejection aims to hurt, tear down and kill off. Yes, it has a goal. If it's consistent, or if there is even an appearance of it, it can make one feel unworthy, causing you to deny your worthiness. It is to encourage you to draw into a state of aloneness and aloofness persuading you to resist love. But your validity is wrapped in the love that has already been given to you. Hidden behind the shadows of rejection; poking, pushing, wrestling to break through the noise of its enemy.

As human beings, we are known to repeatedly sabotage our own happiness, our joy, our goals and objectives in life. When things are going oh so well, we act. We ***do* something** to ensure greatness's calamity.

Why? It is either an inherent belief that you don't deserve more, or you're afraid of what the more or better looks like, again denying that you're worthy or incapable of handling that better, more fruitful place.

If our fathers were absent or they miss the opportunities to tell us that we are worthy, there can be a deeply embedded belief that "you don't deserve better."

Why the fathers? You may have asked yourself several times through these chapters. Perhaps I could have addressed this sooner but now is an even more appropriate place. I believe a father's voice give strength, firmness, and power not to be denied, just as a mother give solitude, a gentleness, and a compassion.

When the fathers voice, that constant reassurance, is absent, a woman searches; attempting to fill something that becomes tremendously hard for her to find. She bows to subordination, not in servitude, but in bondage. She can become a slave to the idea that somewhere she will find what she needs, what she is looking for, outside of herself, outside of her own uniqueness and wonderfulness.

She is ultimately looking to be loosed from the brokenness, wanting to be whole through his surrogate in the position of daddy, significant other or lover.

It yields disappointment over and over and over again and she becomes frustrated with relationships and flustered and heartbroken by what looks like happiness and resembles loyalty and love, because vicarious love and validation don't exist.

She can repeat the cycle or fight like a madwoman to get out! Fighting for her confidence, her identity, her

A Reflection From His Validation

love, and she learns to validate herself. She rejects the rejection she feels, the loneliness, the insecurity, the unworthiness, the need for approval and to live up to unreasonable expectations.

We can change what we listen to, what we follow and what we believe. We can move forward with joy and peace of mind and even more, without repeating the same deafening, stabilizing, elusive cycle.

Quiet the noise!!!

Quiet the negativity.

Quiet the doubt.

The unworthy, self-sabotaging rhetoric shut it up!

As I recognized behaviors that would hinder my growth, I acknowledge them and did what was in my power to create new behaviors.

Remember, often others see or recognize things before you see yourself. Listen, and examine yourself, open and honestly. I use the phrase that I heard from one of my instructors "chew the meat and spit out the bones." This simply means to take what you read and what's applicable, the rest do away with.

We can always learn things about ourselves even if it triggers other self-truths not tied to the direct subject. Allow yourself to be challenged beyond what you currently believe. I have set my face to continual self-examination against the truth of my identity, not the criticism of man.

Continual self-discoveries compel further self-examinations. I examine my motivations, my acceptances for things, my rejections of them, the sacrifices, my tolerances, and any elusiveness.

Remembering that I, yes even I, especially I, am not perfect. But l can strive to be a better me, for me and for us. It is then I can project the light inside on to others and know that we are perfect, for one.

We don't have to look for things in areas that are unfruitful and damaging. Just because we have repeatedly failed ourselves by not looking deeper and expecting greater, doesn't mean we have to continue this pattern. You want to continue to move forward in life, your life!

Our life experiences bring growth or decline, you daughter, choose which. All that you decide, all that you do reflects one with whom you share your DNA, your father.

Reflections from His Validation

1. Are you secure in who you are; appearance, personality, attitude, relationships?

   _____
   _____
   _____
   _____
   _____
   _____
   _____
   _____
   _____
   _____

2. Are there areas where you feel you don't meet expectations? If so, what are they?

   _____
   _____
   _____
   _____
   _____
   _____
   _____
   _____
   _____
   _____

3. When you seriously consider it, whose expectations are you trying to meet?

_____
_____
_____
_____
_____
_____
_____
_____
_____
_____
_____
_____

4. Why do you feel you fall short in these areas?

_____
_____
_____
_____
_____
_____
_____
_____
_____
_____
_____
_____

A Reflection From His Validation

5. If you've set these expectations, why have you set them as such?

   _____
   _____
   _____
   _____
   _____
   _____
   _____
   _____
   _____
   _____
   _____
   _____

6. For what reasons would you feel you aren't enough?

   _____
   _____
   _____
   _____
   _____
   _____
   _____
   _____
   _____
   _____
   _____
   _____

A Reflection of My Father

7. Do you rehearse hurtful words regarding yourself?

   _____
   _____
   _____
   _____
   _____
   _____
   _____
   _____
   _____
   _____
   _____
   _____

   7a. If yes, what are those words?

   _____
   _____
   _____
   _____
   _____
   _____
   _____
   _____
   _____
   _____
   _____
   _____
   _____

A Reflection From His Validation

8. Do you believe them?

9. Is there something you recognized that you want to change? If so, what is it?

10. What does this change look like?

11. What would this mean for you?

A Reflection From His Validation

12. How do you feel about what you've written?

_____
_____
_____
_____
_____
_____
_____
_____

Here are the three most important questions of all these.

13. Is there anyone that can change this but you?

_____

14. Are you willing to change it?

_____

15. Lastly, how are you going to change?

_____
_____
_____
_____
_____
_____
_____
_____

YOUR Words Are the Ones That Matters!

Epilogue

It may take some time before you discover why you lend yourself too often to paralyzing experiences. Why paralyzing? Well, as a result, they can literally STOP (stall, thwart, obstruct, prevent) you from moving forward.

I want you to notice what's happening by defining what **STOP** means.

Stall–to bring to a standstill; check the progress or motion of; especially unintentionally.

Thwart–to oppose successfully; prevent from accomplishing a purpose, to frustrate or baffle.

Obstruct–to block or close up with an obstacle; make difficult to pass; to interrupt, hinder, or oppose the passage, progress, course, etc., of. To block from sight; to be in the way of.

Prevent–To keep from occurring, avert; hinder, to hinder or stop from doing something.

I hope you're paying close attention. Stopping can happen temporarily or indefinitely, in one area or many.

If you stop moving forward that means no growth, no maturing, no deliverance, no healing, no victory, no testimony, no teaching, no encouraging, no ripe fruit, no nurturing and no bringing forth life.

But the most wonderful thing is that we can do something to change it. We don't have to keep repeating the same deafening, stabilizing, illusive cycle!

The meaning of STOP is two-fold. The first is defined as being hindered. The second is to keep from allowing a process to continue.

As I recognize my own behaviors that have hindered my growth, I must acknowledge them to do what is necessary to create new behaviors that would support healthy choices for peace of mind and a joyful life.

We shouldn't have to demand love from someone who doesn't know how to give it, and we don't have to look for validation in areas that are unfruitful, damaging, or settle for the reason of repeatedly failing ourselves by not looking deeper and expecting greater.

Albeit you've done it before, it doesn't mean we have to continue this pattern. You want to continue to move forward in life, your life!

Epilogue

Know that you are beautiful, whether you believe it or not.

Know that you are worthy, whether you believe it or not.

Know that you are valued, whether you believe it or not.

Know that you are loved, whether you believe it or not.

Know that you are enough, whether you believe it or not.

Know that you are treasured, whether you believe it or not.

Know that you are uniquely and wonderfully made, there is no one else like you.

Some may try to compare. Some may come close, but no one, absolutely no one is like you, and that my friend is the truth and is enough. Whether you believe it or not.

Start telling yourself these things. Repeat that you are enough until you start believing it. Even if you may have missed it early on doesn't mean it's too late. Reflect, review, restructure and substantiate your life. Tell yourself, "I am more than enough."

We used to practice an "identity building" exercise we called the mirror exercise (I've also heard motivational speakers refer to their version of this.) The mirror effect calls for you to look in the mirror and make positive declarations about yourself. The declarations would often be contrary to our own negative beliefs about whom we were or what we have been told we were.

When you look at you, you can change you. Engaging in this exercise helps you target the false decrees over your life. All the internal noise can be shut down, mortified, put to death! What you speak over yourself can drown out the noise of what you've been trained to believe if you're intentional and speak it enough. Start making positive declarations over your life.

I don't want to veer from the light of our main subject to far or too long so let's get back to this before we close out this chapter.

A father's voice is loud in our ears. Their words ring in our minds long after their spoken, and our hearts are forced by the power of reverence to believe them.

We soak it in. Every bit of it. We become convinced that what our father said is the way it is. He prepares us for what's to come and teaches us how to receive it.

This is why it is crucial for him to understand the impact of his words, especially speaking to his daughter in their most fragile and impressionable stages of life.

The light of our fathers helps us to shine our own light, even as the moon reflects the sun. A reflection from Marianne Williamson, *Our deepest Fear* (1992) and Moore, C., Hammond, F., Latimore, K., & Wells, K. *Uncovered/Covered* (2006).

Lights are illuminative. They are the revelations you receive and a sign of the dark or unknown places being brought to light. In this case, they are what you discovered reading the chapters.

Shadows can be something that has lingered and followed you for days, months or years. The moment you think you've escaped, they cast taunt after taunt. Here, they represent what you held onto over the years that keep you constrained.

In the exercise below, I would like you to think about what each chapter revealed to you. Go back and look at your answers to the questions if you need to and record your shadows and light from each section.

Example:

Light of Reflection

Shadow	Light
Not seeing my beauty	Realizing that I am beautiful

Light of My Story

Shadow	Light
The illusion of self-fulfillment	Creating my own happiness

Repeat this format for own lights and shadows until you get through the chapters.

Light of Reflection

Shadow   Light
_____   _____

Light of My Story

Shadow   Light
_____   _____

Light of Identity

Shadow   Light
_____   _____

Light of Destined a Daughter

Shadow   Light
_____   _____

Light of His Presence

Shadow   Light
_____   _____

Light of His Love

Shadow   Light
_____   _____

Epilogue

Light of His Validation

Shadow   Light

_____   _____

Now, in the same context, look at what you thought you were or told you were, and counter that with an I am of what you are or will be as you go through this process.

Example:

I am not <u>weak</u> I am <u>strong</u>
I am not <u>afraid</u> I am <u>fearless</u>

<u>*Chapter 1*</u>
    I am not _____ *I am* _____

<u>*Chapter 2*</u>
    I am not _____ *I am* _____

<u>*Chapter 3*</u>
    I am not _____ *I am* _____

<u>*Chapter 4*</u>
    I am not _____ *I am* _____

<u>*Chapter 5*</u>
    I am not _____ *I am* _____

Chapter 6
I am not _____ *I am* _____

Chapter 7
I am not _____ *I am* _____

Look at all your I am's and write them out here.

I am _____
I am _____
I am _____
I am _____
I am _____
I am _____
I am _____

You have just written your personal declaration that you will confess over your life every day, for as long as you need to until you believe it. Until you trust it. Until you live it.

References

All Scripture references are from the Holy Bible, KJV

Frost, Jack (2010) *Experiencing the Fathers Embrace*. Shippensburg, PA: Destiny Images Publishers, Inc.

Williamson, Marianne (1992) **Our Deepest Fear**. From *A Return To Love: Reflections on the Principles of A Course in Miracles, city 1992* Ch. 7 : Work, §3 : Personal Power, p. 190 (p. 165 in some editions) New York, NY. Harper Collins Publishers, Inc.

Moore, C., Hammond, F., Latimore, K., & Wells, K. (2006) **Make Me Like the Moon.** On *Uncovered/Covered* [CD] Laface Records, LLC Records (2016)

CPSIA information can be obtained
at www.ICGtesting.com
Printed in the USA
LVHW051802040220
645815LV00011B/1032